2/02

D0206364

WHEN MEN WERE
THE ONLY MODELS WE HAD

Personal Takes

An occasional series of short books,

in which noted critics write about the persistent

hold particular writers, artists, or cultural

phenomena have had on their

imaginations

WHEN MEN WERE

THE ONLY MODELS WE HAD

My Teachers Barzun,

Fadiman, Trilling

———

Carolyn G. Heilbrun

PENN

University of Pennsylvania Press Philadelphia

Copyright © 2002 Carolyn G. Heilbrun
Printed in the United States of America on acid-free paper

10 9 8 7 6 5 4 3 2 1

Published by

University of Pennsylvania Press

Philadelphia, Pennsylvania 19104-4011

Library of Congress Cataloging-in-Publication Data

Heilbrun, Carolyn G.

When men were the only models we had : my teachers Barzun, Fadiman,

Trilling / Carolyn G. Heilbrun.

　　　p. cm. — (Personal takes)

Includes bibliographical references and index.

ISBN 0-8122-3632-7 (acid-free paper)

　　1. Heilbrun, Carolyn G.—Knowledge and learning.　　2. New York

(N.Y.)—Intellectual life—20th century.　　3. College teachers—United States—

Biography.　　4. Authors, American—20th century—Biography.　　5. Intellectuals

—United States—Biography.　　6. Role models—United States—Biography.

7. Feminists—United States—Education.　　8. Women authors, American—

Education.　　9. Columbia University—Biography.　　10. Trilling, Lionel,

1905–1975.　　11. Fadiman, Clifton, 1904–　　12. Barzun, Jacques, 1907–　　I. Title.

II. Series.

PS3558.E4526 Z477　·2001

378.1′2′092273—dc21

[B]　　　　　　　　　　　　　　　　　　　　　　　　　　　2001034695

Again — to Susan Heath

good editor, good friend

CONTENTS

For George Eliot "the burden and the complexity of
womanhood were not enough; she must reach beyond the
sanctuary and pluck for herself the strange bright fruits of art
and knowledge. Clasping them as few women have ever clasped
them, she would not renounce her own inheritance—
the difference of view, the difference of standard—
nor accept an inappropriate reward."

VIRGINIA WOOLF

ONCE UPON A TIME

*The critic of the opposite sex will be
genuinely puzzled and surprised by an attempt to
alter the current scale of values, and will see in it not merely
a difference of view, but a view that is weak, or trivial,
or sentimental, because it differs from their own.*

VIRGINIA WOOLF, "Women and Fiction"

ONCE UPON A TIME there were three men who exemplified, without knowing it, my ideal life. All of them became famous as writers, influential thinkers, and public figures. Their names are Clifton Fadiman, Lionel Trilling, and Jacques Barzun. They met in college, they remained aware of one another—as friends or, if less than friends, companions and fellow crusaders on behalf of similar ideals. What I recount here is only part of their story, a small part of their significance, their accomplishments. They, however, were a large part of my story, and the place they occupied in my life is what I have set out to convey here. Although one of them never knew of my existence, the second ignored it, and the third treated me with formal kindness, without them I would have had no concrete model in my youth of what I wanted to become.

Indeed, until I was past forty they remained my guides. It is hardly too much to say they were my motivation, my inspiration, my fantasy. Theirs was the universe in which I wished to have my being. When I first encountered them, however, the fact that no woman could have her being in the world where they prevailed evaded my consciousness; the impossibility of that particular dream did not present itself to me as an inexorable fact. Like women before me, I hoped against all evidence that I, an exception, might join that blessed circle. Had it not been for the women's movement of the twentieth century's last three decades, I would have had to choose, as women in academia and elsewhere had long chosen, between my inevitable exclusion from this brilliant, beckoning world or my half-life as an "exceptional" woman —never a full member of these men's fellowship but clinging to the edges of it.

Fadiman, Trilling, and Barzun were, when it came to women, men of their time, at least in their published sentiments. All three of them witnessed the early years of the women's movement, although Trilling died soon after the explosive beginnings of modern feminism. Yet neither Barzun, who has lived into the twenty-first century, nor Fadiman, who missed that turning point by only half a year, took serious notice of women's new place in their universe. The question for me now, in the light of the failure of even these two to change profoundly, is why did I revere only men then, and why those three? Why do I remember my veneration of them as the single most compelling passion of my youth?

Lovers are supposed to serve as milestones, as markers on the road to maturity or old age; if not lovers, then jobs, children, marriage, adventures of one kind or another. But for me Fadiman, Trilling, Barzun are the markers; they were the significant events. Oddly, even when I finally understood that I could never be a colleague in their eyes, my admiration for them, my devotion to them, if qualified, did not abate. Even today, I remember my preoccupation with their world, or what I glimpsed of it, exactly as if these three men had been a palpable part of my life rather than actors in my dream—a dream not of romance but of vocation.

"How do you feel writing about guys?" a friend asked me when I told her about this book. It was a fair question. At the start of my professional life I had written about guys—Edward, Richard, and David Garnett, as well as Christopher Isherwood. True, a woman, Constance Garnett, had been included in my Garnett family history, but through no venture of mine: she simply belonged there, with her group of guys. But thereafter I wrote only of women, their writings, their lives, their status in the world, earlier and now.

Yet, before that time, of course I wrote about guys, and thought about guys, and read as a guy: what else was possible? If I wanted a prototype, an example of the sort of career and accomplishment I sought, where was there to look except at men? True, at Columbia where I studied and taught, as at most other universities, there were a few women professors, but they tended toward type. As we callow students saw it then, they were unmarried, hence unloved—that they might have loved women did not so much as occur to us—and while that fact alone did not disturb me, who had few illusions even then about marriage as the only suitable destiny for women, the sense of their incompleteness was palpable. If we assumed that their apparent unfulfillment arose from their single state, we had no other terms in which to describe what we observed. Now, I can perceive that the wound those women displayed did indeed have to do with deprivation of their womanhood, but not sexually or maternally. The deprivation arose from their having, of necessity, determined not to act or write as women. They had become what I would later call honorary men; they presented themselves and their ideas in male attire. One did not choose them as models; the aura of deficiency was too tangible.

So guys it had to be. They filled my imagination; they occupied all the room in my mind devoted to hope, ambition, emulation. And, what is more, they continued to hold sway over me even after feminism had rescued me both from the hope of becoming one of the boys and from the realization of that role's high cost. When it had become possible to be a woman among women, to have women friends and colleagues, to speak, teach, read, and write as women, their magic still prevailed.

Having placed these men and their accomplishments as the exemplars of my aspirations, I was asked if I ever desired them sexually, ever had fantasies about them in that role. Strangely enough, I never did, either at first encountering them, or in the years since. Those casting a disbelieving eye at this response have asked why not? There are a number of possible reasons. I never at any time in my life was attracted to older men; every man for whom I felt desire was close to my own age; these men were over twenty years my senior. Also, if the longing for a nurturing father explains a woman's passion for older men, having had a supportive father all my early life perhaps enabled me to escape this route toward infatuation. Another possible reason: I was married, and not, as they say, on the hunt. Not long after beginning my graduate studies, I had a child and, soon after, two more. A life as busy as mine hardly left time for sex, let alone sexual fantasies. (I have since learned that this configuration of time and sex under those circumstances is far from universally true; nonetheless, it was true for me.) The main reason, however, is simplest of all: I needed them as exemplars, not as lovers. Freud had written that men experience ambition and the erotic as separate desires; women experience only erotic desire. For me, in this case (pace Freud), it was with those men only the ambitious desire that operated.

But surely I felt affection for them, however expressed or experienced? Not even that. They were beyond affection from such as me: admiration was what they deserved and what they got. What made their gift to me greater, I now believe, than any with which they endowed their male followers was the fact that I knew I could not become like them. When the women's movement finally freed me from the choice between playing at being male or remaining outside the boundaries of male accomplishment, I combined what I had learned from them with the pleasure of thinking and writing as a woman. The male acolytes merely imitated their models and, I suspect, inevitably fell short. For my three guys were not readily imitated, and in the nick of time I was enabled to understand this and not to try to become them, in however pale or awkward a replication.

I had wanted to be a doctor for most of my childhood; specifically, I wanted to be like Banting and discover the equivalent of insulin. At college, an aptitude test revealed my capacities for the law. But women were not welcome in either of these spheres in the 1940s, and it was literature—reading—that occupied and restored me, though it took me a while to admit this, despite the fact that I had been enthralled by books as long as I could remember. (I'm always amazed today to discover that perfectly bright children, even those with highly educated parents, have not yet learned to read fluently even by the age of eight. Probably the regime in schools has changed, or perhaps television, computers, video games render reading inessential.) For me, as for so many then, there was reading and there was life, and they neither competed with nor noticeably affected one another. Fadiman, in *Reading I've Liked*, would insist that "commuters' wives—there are tens of thousands of them—were not really in any active sense doing any reading at all. They were taking their daily novel in a numbed or somnambulistic state. They were using books not for purposes of entertainment, but as an anodyne, a time-killer, a life-killer."

I shall consider this condemnation later, in the light of Fadiman's prevailing and consistent scorn for women in his literary world, but for now let me say that, whether or not this kind of reading is true of "commuters' wives," it was not true of me. Nor do I think it is true of many child readers: we read, I think, to peek outside the boundaries of our world, eventually to step outside those boundaries, but not by means of fantasy or mainly for escape. Rather, I think, with the intentions of explorers, psychologists, and archaeologists, children seek not anodynes but more examples of a moral language than a child's life can give them. I fear that the moral ideas—in the largest sense of moral—that children today receive from videos, television, and computer games are hardly concerned with truth, trust, courtesy, or personal courage in any subtle sense. But, being old, I try to refuse the temptation to damn the occupations of youth—a temptation neither Trilling nor Fadiman resisted; Barzun has contented himself with damning most of the twentieth century and trying to rescue the English language and the ideals of art from decimation.

And so, like many young people who "live in books," I got a job in publishing, about which the less said the better, although publishing in those days had not yet become the property of corporations mainly producing almost anything but books. Then one day in 1949 my husband and I were in Chicago; having already visited the site where he had attended midshipman's school in World War II, we went to look at the University of Chicago. We sat on the grass in the "midway" between the Gothic buildings, and I became convinced that I must go back to school and study literature. We lived in New York, which meant, at least to me in those days, Columbia. I had no intention of continuing for a Ph.D. I would get an M.A. I was merely putting my toe in.

In that first year at Columbia, I attended many lectures, though not the ones I signed up for; no notice was taken of any student apart from his or her appearance in a seminar. My seminar was in Modern Studies, the term then encompassing the years from 1890 to 1950 — a rough demarcation. The professor was William York Tyndall, a man frightened of women and devoted to Joyce with a passion equaled only by those dedicated to Freud. Tyndall barely tolerated women students or women writers: recently, I was amused to come across this recollection in a book by Herbert Marder, who was also a graduate student of his:

> [I] decided to work on Virginia Woolf, "women and fiction" — it was then an uncluttered field, without the sludge that encrusted Yeats and Eliot. My adviser at Columbia [Tyndall] said: "Not much mileage in feminism these days. Virginia Woolf was not a political animal. She was a lady, you know — disliked working-men, Negroes, and Jews."
>
> "There are subversive, radical ideas all over her books," I said.
>
> He puffed decisively on his unlit pipe. "E. M. Forster says she was a snob and proud of it — true Brit. Could generate some heat. I think you should go ahead." So it was settled.

Tyndall, however, was not as adamant on the question of women as was Trilling. Later, I would learn that he and Trilling had been classmates at Columbia, and that Tyndall deeply resented Trilling's greater fame. In Tyndall's seminar I joined in the general fascination with Joyce, and in fact did admire some of his stories, and the first half, together with the Ithaca chapter, of *Ulysses*. I played at analyzing Joyce as others play at bridge or chess. Occasionally I wondered why we worked so hard to find out what Joyce had put into his book on purpose to puzzle us, but I hardly mentioned this doubt, even to myself.

The only part of the studies for my master's degree that enthralled me and that would, as a direct result, commit me to doctoral studies was Lionel Trilling's lectures. He spoke as a prophet—no less dramatic a word will suffice. He made acceptable what we believed, but had thought improper to believe. When, for example, he described how Hyacinth in Henry James's *Princess Casamassima* learned the profound pleasure to be taken in large rooms with high ceilings—a pleasure that those who were both poor and revolutionary had told him contained no virtue—we too suddenly admitted the attraction of space and elegance, if not luxury. Hyacinth kills himself because of his inability to resolve the terrible dilemma that had also tortured me and, I suspect, many others: that art was worth experiencing, that the greatest art did not come from the purest minds, that the rich exploited the poor but at the same time made art possible. If all this was too much for Hyacinth, it was also profoundly distressing to me.

I had grown up liberal in my inclinations despite my politically conservative parents. Hyacinth, lonely like me, like me split in his deepest loyalties, revealed to me, through Trilling's analysis, that the essence of literature was in the tensions of the thinking life. Trilling himself embodied tension, though I could not, in those early days, have so identified the energy that flowed from him. It was only twenty-five years after his death that I would learn of what pulled him, first this way, then that, and of the impossibility of reconciling those conflicts. I remember him saying—or perhaps I read it as I began to read everything he had published—how Freud knew that we paid for everything life gave us with more than equal coin. Long before I came to distrust some of Trilling's obiter dicta, I had learned to distrust Freud, because of his views of women and because of the Freudian psychoanalysts I had come to know. Yet, even distrusting Freud, I agreed with him that tragedy is what most marks us if we are thinkers—a central concept of Trilling's worldview.

Never once in anything he said did Trilling admit women to the fellowship of learning. Men were what it was all about, men struggling for some assurance—these were the actors in Trilling's drama. Trilling readily published comments like this:

Truth, we feel, must *somewhere* be embodied in man. Ever since the nineteenth century, we have been fixing on one kind of person or another, one group of people or another, to satisfy our yearning—the peasant and the child have served our purpose; so has woman; so has the worker; for the English, there has been a special value in Italians and Arabs. (*Gathering of Fugitives*, Trilling's emphasis)

Even if Trilling was using "man" to mean humankind, it is still noticeable that on his list of individual subcategories of human beings (exotics, naifs, all of them), we find "woman"—exotic, naive, other—always an object, never the subject.

Usually when Trilling said "we" he meant men like himself, or younger men learning from him. Some years later, Trilling would take a lot of flak for his use of "we," his assumption that anyone reading him was part of his "we." I never was part of "we," and even in my earliest times of infatuation I knew it to be an impossibility. Later, wistfully, I wondered, though not with much hope, if I could somehow persuade Trilling to include women in his intellectual community. I think I always sensed that this was as probable as persuading Orthodox Jews or Muslims to admit women on an equal basis to their religious life.

It astonishes me now to recognize that almost from the beginning I wanted to confront him, to force him to recognize that I, a woman, was, at the least, not prevented from embodying truth, even if I could not embody it for him. It is clear to me now, and was clear then, that when he spoke of woman or others as embodying truth, it was to deny the possibility of their doing so; his only question was where should "man" look for confirmation. I never confronted him, but it was because of the power he had seized over me, and because of the quality of mind and the persuasiveness he demonstrated in his lectures, that I decided to go on for the doctorate. Perhaps, I must have thought—indeed, I remember thinking—one day he will confirm my right to be a part of the struggle he embodied, of the yearning he expressed.

I would, however, soon have to face the truth that there was no chance of women entering into his union of thinkers. Long before the question of admitting women to Columbia College came to be seriously considered, Trilling declared—and his announcements were always widely quoted—no women at Columbia: he liked the idea of a men's college. It was reported that he even opposed a woman's presence at college faculty meetings.

In the early 1950s, the most important event in my years as a graduate student occurred: I was persuaded by a fellow graduate student—a future professor of literature, although he never went on to get his doctorate (which, particularly if one was a published poet, was not absolutely required in those halcyon days)—to apply for admission to the by then famous Trilling-Barzun seminar. Admittance was strictly limited: the seminar was intended to be small, cohesive, and hardworking. I was accepted into the seminar, as was my friend. There was at least one other woman in the group. I tried once, when she and I met many years later, to ask her how many women members there had been, but she flatly dismissed the question by saying she didn't share my interest in such matters; she remains to this day an unflinching deplorer of feminism.

The seminar was carefully structured by its two instructors. I recall this with amusement when I read of seminars these days where the reading list, the schedule, and the conduct of the class are all under the direction of the students; Trilling did not live to know this, and by the time this fashion took hold Barzun was long gone from the university. We read a book each week, and each week one of us wrote a paper discussing that book from any angle we chose.*

My book was *Jane Eyre*. It is strange to remember that in 1953 not

---

* In a footnote in *Teacher in America* the following year, Barzun noted that "In a seminar, each of ten or twelve students does individual research or reading, and reports before the group, who question and criticize. In a colloquium, all the students prepare the same readings and discuss them." It seems clear that the Barzun-Trilling seminar combined the two: we all prepared the same readings, and then made reports before the group who questioned and criticized them.

much notice was taken of *Jane Eyre*. No books by women were studied in the honors courses; yet Trilling and Barzun included Brontë in their seminar, the only woman on the list. I wrote a paper on the contemporary critical reception of the book, a subject often repeated once feminist criticism entered the academy, but I had then launched myself on a maiden voyage, having simply chosen a topic that seemed to provide an opportunity for both research and interpretation. The practice in the seminar, a method firmly established, no excuses accepted, was for the writer of that week's essay to leave a copy of the paper in the library for the other students to read and to give a copy to each of the instructors. We were true library workers in those days. There were few paperback books, no copy machines: one took notes on reserved books and typed papers with carbons. Did we leave a carbon copy in the library, give one of the exalted men a carbon? Did we type out two clean copies, one for each of them? I can recall only that Barzun liked my paper and Trilling didn't, but that hardly registered; they discussed it as though my opinions and ideas mattered. Even more astonishing, they each annotated each paper, making comments in the margin, as no other paper I wrote in graduate school was ever marked, perhaps ever read. The respect they showed for us was invigorating, and full of the promise of what an academic life might afford. Once, I remember, Trilling responded to something I had said or written, and I must have looked troubled. "Did I traduce you?" I remember him asking.

From that seminar I came away with another vision of what I might find in the life of the mind: friendship, intimacy as it existed between Trilling and Barzun, for they were, famously, friends. By "intimacy," I meant a mutual trust, consultations, laughter, conversation, perhaps private or personal, but not necessarily so, above all the knowledge that they were part of the same group; they were "we." Recently I have learned more of that friendship—I did not earlier even know that they had both attended Columbia College—and discovered that it was indeed, as I had imagined it, a close professional companionship such as I would one day know with female colleagues and the occasional male. Did I dream then that I might one day be their friend? I doubt it, except perhaps as an idle fantasy.

Perhaps I hoped to be a disciple. Trilling had disciples, young men whom he honored, supported, took pleasure in; no woman ever played that role in his life. Barzun did not, I think, have disciples in that sense, neither men nor women, but he continued to welcome women into his graduate seminars in history. Barzun, unlike Trilling, did not strike one as a lovable man. This was odd, since Trilling was also obviously distant and disdainful; one sensed, however, that once one was accepted into his affections he could be lovable. Barzun was always kind, but distant, cool—qualities I eventually came to attribute to his Frenchness; but of that, more anon.

Oddly enough from my point of view, a number of Trilling's "disciples" went on to teach, as I did, at Columbia, to gain tenure, as I did, and to be my colleagues. They all idealized him and referred to him often, long after, so I thought, what he had stood for had ceased to be appropriate. None of his disciples could touch him; indeed, I soon determined that their having idolized him had limited them in their achievements and in their dispositions. Even those who did not teach seemed to betray something essential in Trilling: Norman Podhoretz, for example, became a neoconservative whose opinions seemed altogether foreign to Trilling's as I read him.

I remember reading in Trilling's essay on George Orwell in *The Opposing Self* his account of a discussion about Orwell with a student, and the student's remarking that Orwell was "virtuous." This seemed to Trilling exact and profound, as indeed it was. Yet I often thought, in later years, that these younger men, Trilling's disciples, like Trilling himself, could not recognize virtue in a woman or in any but a certain kind of man. I well remember Trilling sadly remarking about Victorian men—he may have been quoting Chesterton—that, since there had for so long been no wars, men were not risking their lives in battle while women were risking theirs in childbirth; this was a failure of their manhood. Long before feminism I disliked having a woman's life defined exclusively by childbirth. But that was what women were for: I read Chesterton who averred that when women ceased to have children there would be no reason for their existence. Trilling might not have put it quite that definitively, but he was prepared to deny women "the peculiar reality of the moral life." "They seldom exist as men exist—as genuine moral destinies," he famously wrote in his 1957 introduction to *Emma*. Nor was that all. "It is the presumption of our society that women's moral life is not as men's," he declared—and certainly "we" women could hardly deny the point at that time. While I longed to convince him of women's "genuine moral destinies," that wish quickly became less a hope than a dream. Trilling's views on women were unchangeable, and in fact never changed.

What he and Barzun, however, could and did teach me in those student years was that to be highly intelligent, persuasive, and knowledgeable as a thinker and writer, it was essential to write readable, clear, elegant prose and to avoid jargon. "Jargon" was their favorite pejorative term; its misuse arose from the inclusion in prose for a general audience of the specific, technical terms of a particular discipline. When it came to writing, even all those years before incomprehensible "theory" took over, Barzun and Trilling taught us how to write without shame or condescension for an audience as intelligent as we, though not perhaps as professionally trained.

They wrote as I wanted to write, but they were not my first or only models in that important skill. My first exemplar in writing was Clifton Fadiman, whose precise but unpedantic prose I had encountered while still in high school. Fadiman had been at Columbia College with Barzun and Trilling—he was born in 1904, Trilling in 1905, Barzun in 1907—and when I was fifteen, he showed me how one might write intelligently while avoiding the traps of excessive erudition and garbled syntax. Fadiman wrote as though he wanted to entertain the reader, and perhaps, by chance, persuade him (there were no "or hers" for Fadiman or Trilling) of the delights of intellect.

Looking back now I can see that these three men identified for me what I aspired to. What other model had I? Rereading their works today has enabled me to identify the distinct aspects of these men's lives and ideas that I early intuited but could not then have accurately delineated. In writing of them here, I am not attempting biographies, and shall use only published, public materials. I wish only to capture, if I can, that ideal of the life of the mind they represented, and the way that model was eventually translatable to a female possibility. All were, as I wished to be and in a sense became, reformers, seeking to change those aspects of society they saw as limiting and diluting. Two of the three men—Fadiman and Trilling—were, like me, Jewish and suffered from that condition in pre-World War II academia. Barzun, born in France, was also, to some slight extent at least, an outsider. I knew none of this when I first encountered them.

Because they all attended Columbia College, because two of them remained at Columbia throughout their professional lives, they provide me, who also devoted my professional life to that institution, an opportunity to construe their accomplishments in the particular conditions and profound limitations Columbia offered. For Columbia produced these three men, two of whom became part of Columbia's establishment, as in turn it produced me, who became a feminist.

It is worth reemphasizing that none of these men was feminist; Barzun alone seemed capable of respecting female accomplishment and eschewing stereotyped views of women. Trilling frankly admitted no interest in teaching women or in considering their destinies beyond the domestic sphere. Fadiman's many anthologies and introductions hardly indicated any devotion to questions of female destiny; indeed, women writers, as we shall see, were his favorite target when he was scattering literary scorn. Yet these three men, all unconsciously, made my professional life possible by representing both what I wished to join and what I needed to struggle against. Since there was no woman inviting me to the destiny I sought, these three stood in such a woman's place. One male model might have become the unwilling mentor of a confused young woman. Because there were three of them, I avoided that trap—the betrayal of the mentor—and scattered my hopes among the triad.

They knew each other well; me they scarcely knew at all.

Now, midway through my seventies, I find myself thinking back, remembering the time when only men seemed able to represent the life a woman not attracted by conventional female destinies might aspire to. I find it possible to keep distinct my views of these men at the time when they held the greatest sway over my mind—the 1950s and '60s—but at the same time I have discovered the urge to ponder their lives beyond those years, when their influence on my thought did not abate even as my judgment of their ideas became more critical, more confrontational. I want to follow them into the time when the modern feminist movement made feasible a career few in the earlier decades could have imagined possible. What were they writing and propounding in those years?

During the heady beginnings of the feminist movement, when being a woman seemed to encourage rather than limit my professional accomplishment, had that revolution which altered my life in any way affected the thought and the writings of my three models? And if it did affect them, how, and to what extent? Trilling was dead at seventy, but Fadiman worked well into his nineties, and Barzun, now in his nineties, has never ceased to publish and to think. What were they thinking in the late years—what had Trilling been thinking before his death? Did they think about women at all, and was I able to follow their interpretations of modern life half as fervently as I had done at the time of my earliest professional aspirations?

From WASPs and Dryden to Jews and Freud

The first two years, then, take the student and show
him a mirror of the world. He not only fills his head with fair
pictures of reality, but he can begin to think with tolerable
good sense about what he himself wishes to do, both
in the next two college years and later on.

JACQUES BARZUN, Teacher in America

THE TRANSFORMATION OF Columbia in the time between Trilling's, Fadiman's, and Barzun's years as students at the college and Trilling's death is certainly dramatic. The fact that similar changes are to be noted throughout American society generally and in academia in particular does not lessen the violence of the change from the English department's tranquil WASPdom through the Marxist, Jewish, Freudian influence of Trilling's day to the general liberalism and the growing force of feminism already pervasive at Trilling's death in 1975 — in short, in "my" day. If we start with those distant years when Joseph Wood Krutch and Mark Van Doren came as students to Columbia in 1915 and extend this period until my retirement from Columbia in 1993, we will find the beginning of that stretch of decades quaint and gentle, and as distant from my Columbia years as though it had in fact occurred two centuries earlier.

Furthermore, to compare the Columbia of Krutch and Van Doren, both as undergraduates and as faculty, to the Columbia of Trilling and his colleagues is to comprehend the shocking change that Trilling's acceptance into the English department represented. He was, of course, their first Jew. But, as it turned out, he was more even than that. True, as Diana Trilling pointed out, had Trilling been named

Cohen, his mother's birth name, he would never have been considered for an assistant professorship.* He was the right kind of Jew.

Krutch and Van Doren were the right, the perfectly connected WASPs. As famous in their time as Trilling would be in his, they both left autobiographies enabling us better to delineate the different worlds these two generations represented. Krutch and Van Doren published their autobiographies when life had not yet been jolted into the revolutions and reversals the next decades would bring, so that their calm presentation of their close to idyllic lives seemed to require neither apology nor justification.

For one thing, when they both came to Columbia College as students they already knew the "right people"; their college entrance was not into an unknown world composed entirely of strangers. All their classmates would, they could assume, be "their kind." And more than that, their happy, uncomplex, midwestern small-town childhoods (as they, in any case, reported them) had left them with expectations of further ease, however hard they might need to work, and their expectations were satisfactorily fulfilled. Their careers at Columbia were from the beginning smooth, rewarding, and devoid of crucial conflict.

Let us follow them a bit more closely, Krutch first. He enjoyed, as he himself recorded, "two important advantages." First, a colleague of his from Knoxville, Tennessee, was able to recommend Krutch to the colleague's old friend, William Peterfield Trent, "one of the most distinguished and influential of the Graduate faculty who took me more or less under his wing." The second advantage resulted from his soon meeting and developing a lifelong friendship with Mark Van Doren. Mark's brother Carl was "one of the most respected members of the Graduate English teaching staff"; he offered Krutch the perk of his intimate advice and encouragement. From the college, where Krutch sheltered under these two wings, to the graduate school was a mere step. He finished the required courses in two years, and was given an appointment as instructor in Columbia College.

---

* For many years at Columbia, as I well remember, it was falsely rumored that Trilling had changed his name from Cohen to hide his Jewishness.

Mark Van Doren's life, before and during his Columbia years, reads to my eyes like something out of a book called, perhaps, *A Happy Midwestern Boyhood*. The next youngest of five brothers, raised in a loving, congenial family, where he enjoyed school, had warm and understanding parents, and so on and so forth, Mark followed his oldest brother, Carl, to New York and Columbia. "As for what lay ahead of me at Columbia," he wrote, "I had the comfort of knowing that Carl was there and had made all arrangements it was possible for him to make."

Trilling and Fadiman too would study at Columbia under what Alfred Kazin in *New York Jew* called "the old triple-named WASPS"—men such as William Witherle Lawrence, George Philip Knapp, Henry Morgan Ayres, Jefferson Butler Fletcher, George Dinsmore Odell, and William Peterfield Trent—but, as we shall see, in a quite different academic ambience. To indicate the influential circle in which these triple-named WASP professors moved, we have Van Doren's report: "I often wondered about the day when three friends called at [Trent's] house and he was not at home. They were Henry Adams, John Hay, and Theodore Roosevelt." When Krutch and Van Doren, still in the three-name tradition, went on to graduate school at Columbia, three of their classmates there also went on to teach at Columbia, "a really astonishing number from one academic generation," as Krutch put it. This group advancement, of course, seemed to occur in the natural order of events. The three colleagues—Emery Neff, Raymond Weaver, and Roy Dribble—had, however, undergone the mild transition of using only two names. The first of these men would have a profound effect on Trilling's Columbia career.

Van Doren's dissertation on Dryden, not unexpectedly, was accepted by Harcourt, Brace and Howe in 1923 without subsidy. In those years, and until after World War II, doctoral dissertations were required to be published, often at the candidate's expense. Trilling's far more famous dissertation on Matthew Arnold would be published by Norton in 1939, who would nonetheless demand a subsidy from him.

Van Doren went on to follow his brother Carl as a reviewer for the *Nation*; he eventually became its literary editor and movie critic. His career beyond Columbia included as well other satisfying publishing and academic endeavors. He ends his autobiography, published in 1958, thus:

> I should not like to think I am complacent, or lucky, or deluded, or merely pleased. It is more positive than that. By some odd chance and for no good reason I am happy. . . . I hope I do not tempt fate when I say I am happy now. Anything can occur, and the worst things have a way of occurring last. I leave them to be what they will. I speak only of time gone. It went well, and I would be unfair to fate if I denied it.

In fact, one of the "worst things" did occur. Van Doren's son Charles had, in the family tradition and to no one's surprise, started teaching English at Columbia College as one of his father's colleagues. Then, as Mark Van Doren reports it at the end of his autobiography, "in the winter of 1956–57 [Charlie] took part, simply for fun at first, in a quiz program called " 'Twenty-One.' He answered endless questions and made fantastic sums of money; but the notable thing was that something like thirty million listeners fell in love with him." A few years later, after the appearance of his father's autobiography, Charlie turned out to have been given the answers, to have agreed to cheat, to have lied to the grand jury once these facts became known — in short, to have betrayed all in the way of integrity that had seemed to mark his and his father's inheritance. (The whole sad episode was resurrected in the 1990s with the movie *Quiz Show*.) Charlie was finished at Columbia. It was a shocking but, to those of us who resented what we saw as their complacency, somehow not unfitting end to the reign of the Van Dorens at Columbia. Mark Van Doren may have left "the worst" to be what it will, but one cannot suppose he ever imagined that particular worst. The WASP assumption of natural domain had reached its limit.

There is, to me, an amusing footnote to this. In 1962, Fadiman, writing in his anthology *Enter Conversing* and praising Mark Van Doren's autobiography and his teaching, added, "When I try to think of what he taught me, I cannot remember a thing. That is as it should be." Why it is as it should be, I don't know. One recalls few specific points from important teachers, but one can usually recall the thrust and tenor of the teachings, as I can recall the lectures of Trilling and the seminar comments of Trilling and Barzun. Yet I too sat in on Van Doren's Shakespeare lectures, and can remember nothing at all except a general ambience of pleasantness.

Trilling's experience at Columbia College and his eventual hiring there as an instructor in 1932 encompassed a far different set of circumstances. Much has been made of the fact that Trilling was the first Jew hired by the Columbia English department, and certainly anti-Semitism played its vital part. The story is a little more complicated than that, however, as most such stories are. Jews were not widely hired by Ivy League universities until after World War II. Diana Trilling does not get this quite right in her article in Commentary, "Lionel Trilling: A Jew at Columbia." She wrote that "the situation of Jews in American universities changed radically" in the years after the war had started. The situation did indeed change, but not quite so soon. As Hannah Gray, not Jewish but a refugee from Hitler, once observed, none of the major universities would accept refugee Jews from Europe onto their faculties. It was for this reason that the New School in New York City undertook to provide academic positions for Jews. Jews were indeed welcome in all parts of the academic world well after the end of World War II, but not earlier.

Once Trilling was promoted to assistant professor in 1939, Professor Emery Neff, who had directed Trilling's dissertation, came to the Trillings' house to say that he hoped Lionel would not use his appointment as a wedge to open the English department to more Jews. Clifton Fadiman, of course, had earlier been told that Columbia already had its Jew in Lionel. Reading Diana Trilling's memoir of those years, I notice that Fadiman was a close friend of them both at one time. He had, in fact, introduced Diana and Lionel to one another—two people called Li and Di must surely meet—and spent some vacations with them. But in later years I find no mention of Fadiman by either Trilling, or of them by Fadiman. Barzun, on the other hand, remained a steady object of Fadiman's respect and admiration and frequently joined him on radio programs.

In 1927, even before Trilling's appointment as an instructor at Columbia in 1932, Mark Van Doren had been invited by Elliot Cohen, the innovative editor of the *Menorah Journal*, to write an essay on his Jewish students. The students Van Doren discussed were Henry Rosenthal, Clifton Fadiman, Meyer Schapiro, John Gassner, Louis Zukofsky, Herbert Solow, Lionel Trilling, and Charles Prager—in the light of their subsequent careers, an impressive group. They testify to the fact that Jewish students, unlike Jewish faculty, were not unknown in the college. Mark Van Doren described in his autobiography the occasion for this article:

> It was not long before I found I had the reputation of being partial to Jewish students. I doubt that I was, yet it is true that among the Jewish students in my classes there were many who fascinated me by their brilliance and by the saliency of their several characters. I accent "several" for it was the variety among these students that impressed me most.... Somehow they did become my friends—so much so that when one of them happened to tell the editor of the *Menorah Journal* about it he invited me to describe them in an article. I did so in 1927, under the title "Jewish Students I Have Known," and those of them I still see tell me I was fairly prophetic as to their futures.... In Clifton Fadiman I noted the gift of mimicry and the fund of knowledge which everybody continues to associate with him.... I reported of Lionel Trilling that he was "sensitive" and "fastidious" and that he "spoke diffidently, with hushed and harmless voice"; I found in him "dignity and grace," and foretold that whatever he eventually did "will be lovely, for it will be the fruit of a pure intelligence slowly ripened in not too fierce a sun."

The *Menorah Journal* had been founded in 1915, styling itself, in the words of Elinor Grumet, as "radical within Jewish circles, but [aiming] for respectability among educated Americans." As Trilling describes its origins in "Young in the Thirties,"

> Henry Hurwitz had started the Menorah Society at Harvard to deal with the sense of exclusion felt by Jewish students, the method being to make them aware of the interest and dignity of the Jewish past, to assure them of, as it were, the normality of the Jewish present, toward which they would, it was hoped, have the attitude of *noblesse oblige*.

Between the ages of nineteen and twenty-five Trilling published in that magazine. Originally committed to the creation of a Jewish cultural renaissance in America, Trilling was neither religious nor Zionist, and eventually turned his attention to the wider circle of intelligent readers. Trilling's self-identification as a Jew, when I learned of it years later, seemed to me in startling contrast to my own desire in those same years to avoid the contemplation or admission of my own Jewishness whenever possible.

But even with his clear Jewish identity, Trilling wrote in 1944, according to Cynthia Ozick, that he "knew of no writer in English who has added a micromillimeter to his stature by 'realizing his Jewishness,' although I know of some who have curtailed their promise by trying to heighten their Jewish consciousness." That Trilling could write this in 1944 when, as Ozick observes with horror, "the German ovens were at full blast," appalls her. I, for one, at that time, would have agreed with Trilling's statement in its entirety. According to Diana Trilling, neither she nor Lionel nor any of their friends seemed to have focused on Hitler's siege against the Jews, nor did Trilling record his responses to Nazism in later years.

I also did not know in the 1950s that Trilling had been a communist sympathizer in the 1930s, as were most New York intellectuals in those years; although Trilling and most of his circle became anti-Stalinists in the 1930s, neither he nor his group deserted their communist ideals. I, unaware of the communism of the '30s, would thirty years later in the '60s move from a largely unthinking liberalism to something more radical. The story of the '60s, how Trilling regarded them, and how they affected his posthumous reputation, comes later.

There are two moments of exceptional importance in Trilling's life at Columbia. The first is, of course, his being hired at all to teach in the English department. The second is his being kept on as an assistant professor. Diana Trilling believed that Mark Van Doren's account of Trilling in the piece on Jewish students as "one of the less commanding talents of his college generation" was an accurate representation of the impression Trilling made in those years. Why Trilling was hired as an instructor remained mysterious to Diana and, probably, to Lionel. How he got his promotion to assistant professor, however, is the stuff of which Frank Capra movies are made. Not only did this promotion mark the division between WASP dominion and a new approach to literature and culture, it also provides a parable about how the combined forces of individual personality and "divine" (that is, administrative) intervention determine destiny. (Alas, the interference of the administration in faculty appointments was to prove, in the years when I was at Columbia, a far more common and less benevolent occurrence.)

With Trilling, it happened like this. As Diana Trilling wrote in "Lionel Trilling: A Jew at Columbia," throughout the 1930s "Jews were people who made the Columbia faculty uncomfortable, Freudians were people who made the Columbia faculty uncomfortable, Marxists were people who made the Columbia faculty uncomfortable." In Trilling, the Columbia faculty was confronting all these terrors. In addition, the department apparently felt that Trilling was insufficiently forceful, too quiet, his voice too "hushed and harmless." Therefore, Trilling was informed that he would not be kept on in the department.

In an astonishingly uncharacteristic moment, Trilling responded to his dismissal by declaring that in getting rid of him they were getting rid of someone who one day would bring great distinction to the department. Where he had been wont to speak softly, he now shouted, he demanded, he behaved, according to Diana, entirely uncharacteristically. And it worked: he was given another year as an instructor, which eventually extended itself into three years. In 1939 he published his *Matthew Arnold*, and the question of whether he would get tenure had to be faced. There was still no tenured Jew (or Marxist or Freudian) in the English department.

And then what looks like the action of gods disguised as chance operated. Irwin Edwin, a famous (Jewish) professor of philosophy, ran into Lionel on the street and urged him to send a copy of his Matthew Arnold book to the president of Columbia, Nicholas Murray Butler. Butler was a powerful man; he ran the university as a fiefdom; he himself hoped to become President of the United States.

Butler, impressed with Trilling's book, gave a huge, formal dinner party to anoint Trilling—Diana has written about her efforts to discover the correct clothing to wear to so exalted an event, which was white tie; Lionel rented his outfit. And lo, Trilling was on his way to tenure. It is a story that in its mythic qualities appropriately marks the irreversible, stunning transition of the English department from what was essentially a practice of literary appreciation to a more socially oriented reading of texts. True, there was overlap for some years, but the eventual and permanent shift from the old style of literary criticism to the new cultural criticism was never in doubt: Jews, Marx, and Freud were here to stay.

The next essential turnabout would come with the advent of feminism and Trilling's resistance to it, a resistance as ardent as any he had himself experienced years before, and far less mannerly. For example, Trilling, Fadiman, and even more particularly Barzun were to celebrate for many years what came to be called the core courses at Columbia, which Fadiman recalled in *Reading I've Liked*: "The Honors Course was but a systematic extension of the Professor John Erskine educational program. For two years, under the guidance of a group of selected instructors, we read and talked about one great book a week, beginning with Homer and concluding, as I recollect, with William James. That was all there was to the course, and it was by far the most valuable one I took at college." When I, however, joined the Columbia faculty, I was, as a woman, not allowed to teach the so-called honors courses in the college, though I longed to. I cannot resist noting here that, decades later, it afforded me much amusement when the young women now teaching the honors courses, Contemporary Civilization and Humanities (CC and Lit Hum, as they were dubbed), hated almost every minute of it, evidence of the sharp change in the department since the days when those honors courses had been revered.

Years later, when I had left Columbia and long after Trilling's death, I would learn that, despite the feminism he suspected me of harboring, he had voted for my promotion to tenure. I had, in fact, surmised his vote in my favor; I knew enough by the time I achieved tenure to be certain no one in the department would be granted it without Trilling's concurrence. But by then, of course, I no longer retained any illusions about the possibility of a professional relationship with Trilling on any but a technical basis—we were members of the same faculty. Shortly thereafter, Trilling chose to teach only in the college, where, unlike the graduate school, there were not yet any women students, and even our technical alliance was effaced. Columbia was one of the last non-Catholic male schools to become coed, and one of the reasons for this surely was not, as was supposed, the presence of Barnard; it was the powerful protest of Lionel Trilling, which still echoed in all our ears.

There would be other changes in Columbia's English department, sometimes minor but always indicative. Mark Van Doren, for example, has described his oral examination, the summing up of all the class work for the Ph.D., before the dissertation: "This was to be two hours of torture, we all understood, at the conclusion of which a committee of professors would tell us whether our knowledge of English literature was comprehensive enough, and in places deep enough, for us to become doctors of philosophy." Torture it may have been, but the conduct of the examiners, as Van Doren reports it, was gentlemanly in the extreme.

By the time I came to sit as a professor on oral examinations, the students were permitted to pick their own fields and authors upon which to be tested; these selected subjects became narrower and narrower through the years. The fields had not narrowed significantly when I took my oral examination, but the courtesy shown the students in Van Doren's day was gone. I took my orals in the spring; all but one of the professors I knew and had worked with had already departed for the summer. I was examined by strangers who asked unfamiliar questions. The only question I remember came from a medievalist whose name I have happily also forgotten; he asked, "In what language did Ovid write?" Since I could hardly imagine he meant me to answer "Latin," I stared, was indecisive, and was marked down.

As to the defense of the dissertation, Van Doren reports: "The examination in May, in a stately room of what I still call the old library, though that is not its official name, was one of the surprises of my life. The professors — not merely those I had studied with but eminent ones from other departments — rose when I entered the room and did not sit down until I had. This is an age-old custom, and a beautiful one."

I believe, though I have no way of knowing, that Trilling prized some of these "old" customs, as did I. Nonetheless, in his notebooks or journal, he would deplore "such people as Mark VD, who yearly seems to me to grow weaker & weaker, more academic, less a person." I, who admired the "old" customs even as they excluded me, learned that when established values are challenged, however carefully, the courteous, often lovely behavior that accompanied them goes also. At one of the last defenses I chaired at Columbia, a male professor arrived in what appeared to me to be his undershirt. He had clearly not read the dissertation under discussion, and was rude to the other examiners. Needless to say, we did not rise at the candidate's entrance.

As to my own defense, I, like many other women graduate students at Columbia in the 1950s and early '60s, was offered a perfunctory defense and quietly ushered out a back door.*

By the time I received my master's degree in 1951, the old WASPs were for the most part either gone or little in evidence. I did attend

---

* For more details on the experience of feminists in graduate schools, see Gayle Greene and Coppélia Kahn, eds., *Changing Subjects: The Making of Feminist Literary Criticism.*

Mark Van Doren's lectures on Shakespeare, which I enjoyed but found rather mild and, as I have said, forgettable. Shakespeare would subsequently become one of my more private passionate interests, and Van Doren's book on the plays is still in my library. It did not, however, excite me as did other books, even from that less radical time.

Trilling's lectures, on the contrary, seemed to hold the key to salvation, and salvation, for me as for him, was what I hoped to find in literature. Not religious salvation, of course, but a sense of how to live in a culture I both treasured and wished to overturn. What Trilling provided was an acrobatic balance between "bourgeois" values and the need radically to affect them. It was in literature that he believed this balance, and profound instruction on how to live, could be found. I always followed him in this.

Trilling, as we shall see, had been largely formed by the 1930s, a decade that, until the '60s, I had no clear idea of whatever. For me it was the '60s that would bring my own ideas into focus and Trilling's youthful experiences into view. In the very early 1950s, I listened and admired and learned, mostly from Trilling; Barzun I was not to meet until the seminar he taught with Trilling. In those years, for me, the question of being Jewish did not arise. The question of being a woman in that academic world was seldom out of sight or thought, although never discussed with Trilling, with my peers, or indeed, with anyone at all.

CLIFTON FADIMAN

*This collection is compiled by a reading enthusiast
and will probably be read by others whose inclinations
are somewhat similar.*

CLIFTON FADIMAN, Reading I've Liked

ALTHOUGH FADIMAN was the first met of "my" three men, I encountered him only on the pages of a book. If I came to know Trilling
and Barzun not only through their books, or eventually, in the seminar
room, Fadiman's earlier influence was in no way less profound. Trilling's classes, first and always, were lectures to large audiences, silent
and enthralled: no student participation. I did not encounter Barzun,
the historian, until the Barzun-Trilling graduate seminar. After that,
I think they both recognized me as a person with a name and an identity—a graduate student, in danger of being feminist, although in
1953 none of us had heard that word in common usage. Apparently
my vocation, as I came to think of it, was evident to them before it
was to me.

Fadiman would never have recognized me, although I could readily,
some years later, have identified him: he was often photographed, for
his book jackets and in connection with his radio show *Information
Please*. What he assured me of, even when I was fifteen, was his evident
conviction, his frequent demonstration, that a writer could, like him,
be both intellectual, even "highbrow," and yet available to those who
did not think of themselves as either but who found discussions of
ideas and books intriguing. I knew from an early age that I wanted to
be that kind of writer; he was the example demonstrating the possibility of that desire. In short, if I could write like him I might become

professional like him; I too might be an intelligent and engaging commentator on literary matters.

Trilling always wrote of "we": indeed, he became, in certain circles, notorious for this habit, for statements such as, "We" do not go to the movies any more. Barzun sometimes wrote prescriptively to "you" but, as I hope to show, usefully and forgivably. Only Fadiman regularly spoke of "I," telling of his experiences as a reader and reviewer, writing of how he had come to be in that place where we found him, reviewing the books he was recommending to us. So though I never spoke to Fadiman, he spoke to me first of the three, and most persuasively: he embodied a tone, a way of knowing his audience and warming to it. Unlike Trilling and Barzun, whose tone awed me for years, Fadiman spoke in a voice I could respond to, could dare to claim, could hope to claim.

Fadiman wrote, in *Reading I've Liked*, what he assured us would be his first, last, and only venture into autobiography. As far as I know, he kept his word about that on the whole, although, as we will see, there were to occur occasional forays into retrospection. Trilling, dead two decades earlier than the others, was unveiled by his wife but left only the barest notes toward an autobiography. Hints about Barzun's early life appeared in an essay he published, most satisfactorily, I thought, in a collection of *Living Philosophies* edited by Fadiman in 1990. Of Barzun, the one of the three I spoke to most often, even met up with for lunch from time to time, I now know least. Diana Trilling has published a history of her and Lionel's marriage, and Fadiman's daughter, Anne, the editor of *American Scholar*, has written delightfully and lovingly of her father. Anne Fadiman's book Ex Libris appeared in my life at the same time as the news of her father's death; it was a moment that marked my reacquaintance with Clifton Fadiman.

Fadiman's was the life I thought I might live, his the writing that suggested how I might myself one day write. I could never be Trilling or Barzun, could not even be, as Fadiman knew he could not be, a "real" professor, let alone one capable of following in their footsteps. Fadiman, he insisted in *Reading I've Liked*, had become a popular commentator on literature rather than a scholar, or a professor, or what he would insist he was not, a "critic," because he wasn't qualified for these more exalted positions. Repeatedly referring to himself as only a "reviewer," he never acknowledged that, in fact, he had been denied the chance to be a scholar and critic, not because of any limitation of his own but rather as a result of a decision by Columbia's English department. Certainly, if we are to believe Alfred Kazin, Fadiman's explanations of the pattern his life followed do not quite describe the case.

As Kazin reports in *New York Jew*, the English chairman had told Fadiman at graduation, "We have room for only one Jew, and we have chosen Mr. Trilling." Even if these were not the chairman's exact words, Fadiman well knew the situation: what Kazin dubs a "department as crowded with three-barrelled Anglican names as the House of Bishops." He turned his eyes elsewhere. As in all his writing he never once admitted that he might indeed have qualified for the high intellectual life he liked to call himself unsuited to, neither can I remember an instance when he mentioned being Jewish.* I now understand that Fadiman's failing to mention that he had missed out on the academic life because he was Jewish is similar to my failure as a woman in my early years in graduate school publicly to admit to any serious academic intentions.

Diana Trilling reveals in *The Beginning of the Journey* that "Several of Lionel's college friends, Fadiman among them, would very much have wanted the appointment; the fact that it went to Lionel was always a source of bitterness to Kip." (Fadiman was called "Kip" by all who knew him.) As Fadiman pursued his chosen profession of reviewer, Trilling in his turn felt bitterness toward Fadiman: as Diana tells it,

---

*Interestingly, Anne Fadiman mentions that her father "grew up in Brooklyn in an immigrant family too poor to take him to a restaurant until he reached his teens, but not too poor to fill two black-walnut bookcases with the likes of Scott, Tolstoy, and Maupassant." Yet she also tells us that she is descended from Jews, Presbyterians, Episcopalians, Mormons, a Christian Scientist, and a Catholic, eliding the fact that she is half Jewish. Probably Fadiman did not claim a Jewish heritage any more than did I in those years.

Lionel "had before him ... the discouraging example of Kip Fadiman's quick rise to literary recognition. On the basis of but a few pieces for the *Nation*, Fadiman had become in the early thirties the most enviously noticed critic of our generation."

Trilling and Fadiman did, however, remain friends. We learn from Trilling's notebooks that it was Fadiman who passed on to Trilling a letter from Hemingway, a writer much admired by Trilling. Fadiman, reviewing *The Liberal Imagination* in the *New Yorker* in 1950, observed that "Lionel Trilling bears, doubtless with fortitude, the most aggressively euphonious name of any writer since Edna St. Vincent Millay. He also, it seems to me, owns and operates one of the most adequately equipped critical intelligences in the country."

When Fadiman reached fifty, he tells us in *Party of One*, a collection of his reviews, he took stock of what he knew he would never do or be. His words, ringing with clarity and pain, mark that moment in each life nearer to death than to birth. At that age, one knows there are roles in life one will never play. For me, the dream of being a doctor, never very practical or examined, was released. Fadiman, too, may have had a reverie, now abandoned:

"I have always dreamed, among other things," he wrote,

of being a scholar, perhaps even a college professor. These callings seem to my mind far more exciting than the most glamorous of Mr. Mitty's secret lives, involving as they do the never-ending risk of working amid ideas, which are really dangerous. The airman at most kills himself but a bad idea can kill tens of millions. It has done so and is doing so.

I do not have enough brains to be a scholar—I mean a good scholar—and that's about all there is to it. But I can now see that the Mitty in me has in part dictated my life. My Mitty, at turn after turn, has urged me toward activities that have resulted in my becoming a kind of hemi-demi-semi-professor, or perhaps only a hemi-demi-semi-quasi-professor. For about a quarter of a century I have been one of that small, unimpressive army of American communicators who act as middlemen of thought and opinion. (I have also engaged in several televisionary enterprises that did not impinge on thought or opinion in any way. One must live. So—I speak as a married man and father of three—must five.)

I have been a kind of pitchman-professor, selling ideas, often other men's, at marked down figures, which are easier to pay than the full price of complete intellectual concentration. I do not apologize for this. It is the best I and my many peers can do. And I am convinced the job is necessary.

This confession is among the saddest and most wrenching of any I know. Sad, even though he was a great success in his role of "pitchman-professor"; wrenching because one can hear the pain, and the generosity that does not belittle the goal he was denied. Ironically, I had become the professor he could not be: I had wanted to become what he became, and instead achieved the role he would have chosen. We had changed places, we had entered one another's visionary territory. Not, of course, that Fadiman knew anything of this, or, until recently, that I did. Nor do I suggest that I was as good a professor and scholar as he would have been.

I wish I could remember whether, discovering *Reading I've Liked* at fifteen, I had found it in the library or read my mother's copy. I rather think the latter, since I have the sense of having read and reread this book in a way suggesting its continuous presence. My mother was a great reader, and I read what she read. In time these roles would be reversed: once I had graduated from college and moved back to Manhattan, I began to supply my mother with books, including those I borrowed from the New York Society Library. The only glitch in those years of my ferrying books was when I left her with Philip Roth's *Portnoy's Complaint*. She telephoned me the next day to say I must come get the book, remove it from her house; it was loathsome and, apparently, likely to pollute the very air. My mother was a broad-minded reader and a largely unblushing viewer of life, but with that book she had reached her limits. To this day I do not know whether it was the sexual details or the mother-hating that so upset her. But, her and Portnoy's complaints aside, we read books together and spoke of them, and together mulled them over in conversations, with intensity and laughter. When, in 2000, I acquired a secondhand copy of Fadiman's first book, I was glad to see it contained food stains and marginalia, in keeping with his and his daughter Anne's views that books should bear evidence of having been lived with.

Fadiman's life after college early indicated the path he would follow as a reader and judge of new books. He became an editorial assistant in a small publishing house where he was forced to read endless manuscripts of novels by unknown authors who could neither write nor structure a work of fiction. He wished there were a way to discourage these hopefuls before so much publishing time was wasted in reading their submissions. How could he have imagined today's publishing world, owned and controlled by manufacturers of non-book products who rarely care to read beyond the bottom line?

Indeed, his comments on some aspects of the literary life in his day read rather oddly now, sixty years later. He observes in *Reading I've Liked* that "Today the universal appeal of our Western tradition is readily acknowledged." Had he joined Trilling as a professor at Columbia, the struggle to expand the Contemporary Civilization and Humanities courses at Columbia beyond the Western tradition would have amazed and disturbed him. He regrets, also together with Trilling, that reading aloud is a forgotten habit. Of course, taped books, which so many of us listen to when traveling by car, suggest that lost habits are often revived in unforeseen ways. But if many of Fadiman's obiter dicta are dated, that is because as a reviewer he had to confront the new; he had to reach his own judgments about what was being published, and inevitably time might render some of those judgments mistaken. Trilling and Barzun, on the other hand, safe in their academic harbor, were free to deal with already acclaimed writings, free to take long views and compose them in a leisurely manner, without weekly or monthly deadlines.

Yet Fadiman was clearly a man who treasured literature, a man who, like me, had read from the age of four and could not imagine a life without reading. So I might hope to be a reviewer, not a literary critic, which at fifteen I did not consider a possible fate; I had hardly read any literary criticism; Fadiman, in *Reading I've Liked*, explained to me why only reviewing was suited to us both: "Literary criticism is an art, like the writing of tragedies or the making of love, and, similarly, does not pay. Book reviewing is a device for earning a living. . . . Some sort of sieve has to be interposed between printer and public. The reviewer is that sieve, a generally honest, usually uninspired, and mildly useful sieve." I thought at that time that being such a sieve was not a bad aim in life, and perhaps that is, in a way, what I have become. Instead of reviewing books, however, I studied them for hints as to what women had been, what they might be, and how, albeit with men as then the only available models, the moral life might be understood. If not Fadiman's sort of sieve, I have served as a transmitter of ideas on questions concerning gender, and do not, compared to feminists such as Joan Scott or Toril Moi, claim the mantle of literary or historical critic.

And there was no delight greater than the discovery that the marvelously erudite Mr. Fadiman (his pose of modesty did not, young as I was, fool me for a moment) did not like *Madame Bovary* any more than I did, or *Great Expectations* any less:

> Serious students of literature would doubtless rank *Madame Bovary* as a more significant work of fiction than *Great Expectations*. . . . *Great Expectations* happens to be merely a Dickens novel that millions of plain readers have enjoyed. But for me *Madame Bovary* has no virtues except those of perfection. It is without magic, without personality, it is not rereadable. . . . A lycée-trained Frenchman might have the opposite reaction and be equally unable to defend it.

True, as I became a graduate student and climbed up on my stilts, I learned to praise Flaubert and, under the temporary sway of F. R. Leavis, scorn Dickens, but once past those show-off years, I reverted to my and Fadiman's original opinion. (Leavis, too, changed his mind about Dickens, one of the few instances, I think, when he did reverse himself.) Like Fadiman, I became, with some maturity, what he had, in my youth, declared himself to be: "I must unmask and declare myself at once," he wrote. "My friends, I am that most despised of literary animals, an eclectic."

We might note here that Mark Van Doren also deserted the highbrow stuff, but he waited until he published his autobiography to admit it publicly: he confessed that in the 1940s he had begun reading detective fiction, all kinds; "I read with an undiscriminating appetite." Detective fiction, he added, not wanting to put it on a level with, say, *Madame Bovary*, "has virtues that seemed to me life-saving in those days. It wholly absorbed me, so that I forgot things I wanted to forget; it gave me stories, not the substitutes for stories that fiction of the 'better' sort was cultivating; it preferred good people to bad people, a refreshing thing in times when many writers tell us they have done with the distinction; it suggested that law was admirable, and showed it to be no respecter of persons; it was a riot of fancy."

I did not of course follow Mr. Fadiman in all his tastes; I had my priorities. When in *Reading I've Liked* he scorned the Janeites—admirers, nay adorers, of Jane Austen—"so proud and prejudiced, for whom nothing has happened to the English novel since Miss Austen turned up her genteel toes"—I was not with him. Even before graduate school, I knew that Jane Austen was in no way genteel; I would not even have gone so far as thus to characterize her toes. And it must be observed here, and dwelt upon more fully a bit later, that any time Fadiman wanted to cast aspersions, or find an instance of some regrettable taste in reading, it was always a woman writer to whom he turned for an example. Thus it was that not even Jane Austen, the single female writer adored by patriarchs, escaped the severely misogynist gaze of Fadiman. But, even disagreeing with my unseen mentor about Austen, I had not yet learned the word "misogynist," nor become aware of its flourishes. It did not occur to me that anyone worth extensive study was not a man.

Having forgiven Fadiman for his sneer about Jane Austen, I welcomed him back into my heart four years later when I was in college and he published a volume entitled *The Short Stories of Henry James*. I thought then, and I still think, that this was an admirable and, in 1945, a remarkably advanced and incisive introduction to the Master. Professors would begin to rally around James at the same time; as Fadiman wrote, the greatness of James was beginning to become apparent "to a small group of literary critics and scholars." Certainly it had become apparent to Fadiman's classmate Lionel Trilling, who would expound on James's brilliance in *The Princess Casamassima* at about the same time. (Fadiman praised *The Princess Casamassima* in his introduction to James's stories, apparently unaware of Trilling's simultaneous celebration of that novel.) In a footnote to his essay, which appeared in *The Liberal Imagination*, Trilling deplored the fact that "In a single year James brought out two major works; he thought they were his best to date and expected great things of them; he was told by the reviewers that they were not really novels at all; he was scorned and sneered at and condescended to and dismissed. In adjacent columns the ephemeral novels of the day were treated with gentle respect."

These words are worth quoting here, not only to establish that in the 1940s both men were celebrating and reviving the genius of Henry James but also to notice the distinction Trilling makes between great writers and "ephemeral novels." Trilling's position as a professor of English allowed him to deal only with great writers, while Fadiman, a reviewer, had to judge "ephemeral novels" without the advantage of hindsight to tell him how ephemeral they were. In writing about James, however, Fadiman escaped the charge of temporary notice; his edition of the selected *Short Stories of Henry James*, though it appeared during wartime, had after a decade sold slightly under 60,000 copies.

Jacques Barzun, perhaps before Fadiman and Trilling, played a pivotal role in the Henry James revival. As Barzun recounts it in *The Energies of Art*, in the early 1940s

I casually tried to interest a friend and colleague, now a famous critic, to read a little James. He had once come across the story "Glasses," and on the strength of its weakness was now a declared enemy of its author. I persevered and made him read [further]. My friend was soon converted and shortly became a propagandist in his turn. It was he who persuaded two very influential writers [Fadiman and Trilling?] to reconsider their hostile views and they, through essays and anthologies, led the great revival.

Perhaps I was reading Fadiman's collection of Henry James's stories while I was at Wellesley; modern literary studies at that then staid college ended with James. We were hardly encouraged to read, let alone study, anyone less delicate. Joyce was a definite no-no, and who in the world had heard of Virginia Woolf? I remember that the year after Fadiman published the James stories, my first serious boyfriend— well, that's what we called them then—and I argued about James, whom he found precious and finicky and whom I defended against the more robust Americans dear to his heart. I am ready to have the same debate today.

Since 1945, however, those of us bewitched by the James family have learned much that Fadiman could not know. He tells us, for example, that James "seemed to have had no passionate relationships with men or women," which has turned out to be incorrect, but Fadiman said "seemed." There are a few other suppositions that time would alter. But in the main Fadiman got it right, not least in pointing out to me that James's favorite word was "awareness." It became and has remained the quality I most prize in people, the quality whose lack in them I most profoundly regret. In a poem Yeats had declared that "men (sic) must choose between perfection of the life and of the work." Fadiman suggested that James had chosen the work, although what perfection of the life consisted in few, certainly not Yeats, ever made explicit. I suspected that most Americans thought it meant adherence to what came to be promoted as "family values" (which I distrusted even then, avant la lettre).

Now, in what a character in "The Jolly Corner," the last story in the Fadiman collection, calls "the afternoon of life," I still cherish in the work of Henry James all that Fadiman taught me to appreciate. I still like to think of James as a man to whom nothing happened but who, unlike his John Marcher and his Strether, lived "one of the most active lives of the entire century." Furthermore, I agree with Fadiman, or am assured he would agree with me, that "The Beast in the Jungle" is about John Marcher's failure to love, or to live, and is not, as current theory would have it, about homosexuality. Failure to love can be portrayed in many ways; the story is about personal defeat, not sexual mores or orientation.

As it happened, in later years I would develop an impassioned admiration for Henry's brother, William James, whose philosophy and views on religion I concurred with. In 1983, Jacques Barzun in his exemplary *A Stroll with William James* would elucidate these views for me, and, moreover, observe how close the James brothers were in their conceptions of the world. But William James and Barzun are for a later chapter.

Once Fadiman had flung me into the arms of Henry James, I rather lost my close identification with his opinions; I read his reviews in the *New Yorker*, but with less gratitude and admiration. I had by then become a snooty graduate student and later a busy teacher and mother. We rather lost touch with one another, which is to say he meant less to me and I offered him less adulation. I listened, as did my parents and many other "middlebrows," to *Information Please*, a radio quiz program for regular experts and occasional famous guests, whose spontaneous wit and erudition delighted us all. But here I was to face further disillusionment. The boyfriend with whom I had clashed over Henry James had gone on to get a Ph.D. His dissertation was on Glenway Wescott, to whom he (now friend not boyfriend) introduced me one evening. I remembered having heard Wescott on *Information Please* and complimented him on his cleverness. He told me that, not considering himself clever, he had declined to go on the program, but was assured that he would be given the questions and answers in advance. No one mentioned this at the time of the *Twenty-One* scandal, but then, no money had been proffered, nor had anyone, as far as we know, offered to marry any of Fadiman's experts, as they had Charlie Van Doren.

Now, searching out what Fadiman had been writing during the 1950s and '60s, I find that my former model did not bring himself to my notice during those years. In the early 1950s he began to write monthly essays for *Holiday* magazine; his instructions were, simply, to write about whatever interested him. *Enter Conversing*, the book collecting these essays—which I have lately read—fails even now to engage me. Nor, I think, would the Book-of-the-Month Club, whose Board of Judges Fadiman joined in the 1940s, have meant anything to me in those days. Like so many academics, I joined it only in 1975, when it met my exalted standards with a great bargain. The club operated this way: if one agreed to order four books a year, one could get the free selection on offer. Janice Radway, in her study of the club, explains how this worked for many of us: "By the time I actually mailed the coupon three years into graduate school, I had learned to disparage the club as a middlebrow operation. . . . What I [now] coveted was the *Concise Edition of the Oxford English Dictionary*." And so it was with me. I can't remember what four books I ordered before canceling my subscription, but the *Concise Oxford Dictionary* is still with me and still in constant use. I didn't think about the Book Club again until I read Radway's book—I had admired her study of romantic novels and their readers—and learned that Fadiman had been interviewed about the Book-of-the-Month Club by the Oral History department at Columbia in 1955. He was still a judge for the club at that time, and would serve as one for a total of fifty years.

A perusal of this interview offers relatively little new or startling information. Fadiman refers to some of the books selected by the club, what he thought of them then and thinks of them now. I did learn that he was, in his own words, a "Dickens maniac," as his placing *Great Expectations* above *Madame Bovary* had suggested. He mentions a typical problem in 1953, when the club took two books—"both unexceptional books, sincere and honest, each in its own way, but on the whole mediocre. But they were the best we had, and we just had to take them. We always feel a little unhappy then, but there is nothing else we can do." "I'm the one," he announced later, "who is always talking about whether or not this book will sell or won't sell. You see, I'm an old editor and I'm rather proud of my ability to determine whether a book will sell. I was paid for ten years to get books that would sell for Simon and Schuster, and so I'm supposed to know something about this business."

In the course of the interview, Fadiman confessed to a preference that reminded me why I had chosen him as my model so many years ago: "I have one predilection. Now this will sound terribly snobbish, but I don't mean it to be. I like well written, well bred English novels about intelligent people, as against the hard-fisted, sensational novels written by young Americans full of lavatory wall words. I like people to be able to use the language properly, and I must say that Englishmen use it better than we do." In 2000 I wrote a study of the modern detective novel in which, speaking only of that genre, I said much the same thing. I recognized, as Fadiman surely did, that some Americans use the language properly, but the general rule still prevails. I know, I know, this is a crusty opinion, only tolerated these days, if at all, in old parties like me. But I'm certain Barzun still agrees with Fadiman and me.

Fadiman's interview about the Book-of-the-Month Club reminds me of the long forgotten rumors about him I used to hear in the late 1950s—that he had "sold out," a phrase often on our tongues then; quite meaningless, it probably indicated envy if it signified anything at all. But whatever it meant, Fadiman was a prime example of it. Although qualified for "higher" things, he had gone to work for the Book-of-the-Month Club, earning, gossip said, a salary of twenty-five thousand dollars a year; a lot of money then. We heard (how? from whom?) that he liked good wine and good food and wanted to afford these tastes. I have since read his disquisitions on wine and cheese (a whole book devoted to essays on the former), so perhaps there was something in it. Alas, we thought, here is a man who has deserted literature for a sybaritic life. That we would all have leaped at the chance to be a judge of the Book-of-the-Month Club hardly needs saying.

As must by now have become obvious, the late 1950s were for me a difficult period, busy because, unlike the majority of women then, I worked fulltime while raising three children. My husband helped when asked, but he and all fathers were then without the sort of commitment men now make, or are supposed to make, to childcare and the running of the house. Those years were also a time of the most oppressive conventions; female miseries, most harshly endured in the suburbs but felt by us all, were ready at the touch of a match to explode into the modern women's movement.

About all this, Fadiman would certainly have had nothing to say to me, had I been reading him. I see now that in one of his *Holiday* columns, commenting on Harold Nicolson's *Good Behavior*, he mentions with glee, or so it seems, Nicolson's astonishment at "the position of power we [Americans] grant to our women." It is not easy to decide which of the words in this sentence is the most annoying, but I think I would now vote for "we," and "our," with "power" close behind. But Fadiman on women is the subject of the next chapter.

Even as I mused upon the Fadiman I had first known in his earliest books, he was in a sense returned to me in the writings of his daughter, Anne Fadiman. I encountered her first as a gift; a friend knowing my delight in the perfectly written essay presented me with her collection of essays, *Ex Libris*, subtitled "Confessions of a Common Reader." The phrase "common reader," originated by Samuel Johnson and since claimed by Virginia Woolf, had found a worthy third celebrant in Anne Fadiman. Those who use the phrase wish to be read, above all, for pleasure; her presence in such company suggests the elegance of the Fadiman legacy.

Anne Fadiman's name, indeed her very existence, was first made known to me when she was appointed editor of the *American Scholar*, a journal I had long admired but, together with many others, had abandoned because of its harshly illiberal writers and policies. Renewing my subscription, I was immediately enthralled with my first Anne Fadiman essay, a delightful discourse on larks and owls — larks being those who retire and arise early, owls those who arise late and, inevitably, retire late. Myself an owl, I had long pondered this strange bifurcation within humankind. Ms. Fadiman delineated it perfectly, using, as do the best essayists, examples from both the public and the private sphere. Herself an owl, she is married to a lark; nor is this the only dichotomy their marriage includes. She revels in tales of arctic explorations and adventures, her husband is "a rain-forest man"; she is a winter, he a summer person. She writes of her marriage and her children with a delicious exactness that reveals little that is vital about her marriage, but much about the general disorder of marriage and the irrelevance of agreement on mundane matters. So the details of her existence are transformed, not only into amusement for the reader but also into a lightly philosophical evocation of weighty issues.

Her skill as a writer enchanted me, not least because it echoed, without imitating, the quality of her father's early prose, when he exhibited both profundity and charm before becoming more mechanically clever. Above all, she is without his prejudices, without the barbs, chiefly against women, without the sneers that were unlikely to be challenged when he wrote. Anne Fadiman reports that her father, even at ninety, called all women under eighty "girls"; I was not surprised to hear it. Imagine my feminist pleasure when, in counterpoint to Athena's rising from Zeus' head, Fadiman himself, before my very eyes, was reborn for me from his daughter's head, his misogyny excised.

With her, as with him, "the academic I had once thought I'd be had been forever replaced by the journalist I had become." Was it her experience in what she calls her "bibliolatrous family" that convinced her she was doomed to be an academic? The family were incessant proofreaders even of menus, they collected abstruse vocabulary, and, as Fadiman U, competed against college teams in contests of information on television. Father strove to inculcate memory and literature; of himself he liked to say that he did nothing but think, and this served him well when he became suddenly blind at eighty-eight. He turned to listening to tapes instead of reading and, as ever, to memory. Father and daughter, at the moment he learned he could no longer see, together recalled Milton's sonnet on his blindness.

Daughter Fadiman allows herself personal details that Fadiman would have eschewed with distaste, but as she offers them in these more open times, they only increase our trust in her. Like her father's essays for *Holiday*, these are about what interests her, and she seduces us into her life without our ever wondering why we are there. So I know she was still a virgin at eighteen, that she had a lover in college, how she likes to arrange her books. Nothing had in a very long time offered me a shock of recognition as powerful as when I learned that the only marital intimacy she was reluctant to attempt was the combining of her books with her husband's. Married over half a century, my husband and I still have our special shelves, although we too have combined our copies of mutual favorites.

I celebrate, above all, daughter Fadiman's feminist clarity: "I am, by process of elimination, Ms. Fadiman. I can't be Miss Fadiman because I'm married. I can't be Mrs. Fadiman because my husband is Mr. Colt. I can't be Mrs. Colt because my name is Fadiman. I am, to my surprise, the very woman for whom Ms. was invented." Note the tone, the style, the grace. Which is why Cynthia Ozick, no feminist, and I, feminist to the core, can both enjoy and acclaim Anne Fadiman.

From her subordinate clauses, I learn about father Fadiman's life in the years after I left off regularly reading him—his moves from the east coast to the west coast, then back to east coast, then to Florida of all places. But why should I be surprised? In one of his reviews, he celebrated, indeed defended at some length, his removal from Manhattan to the suburbs. His daughter, I am happy to learn, has reversed the process: the mother of two, she lives in a loft in Manhattan. Where else could such a good writer live? * She does not reveal the facts about her father I had myself garnered from the dedications of his books: that Fadiman was twice married, and that it was his first wife to whom he dedicated the short stories of Henry James and who taught him the delights of food and wine. (I further learned, from Diana Trilling, that "Kip Fadiman assured Lionel that there was only one test of a good marriage, the distance a man could put between himself and his wife." Perhaps he changed his mind about this; certainly Lionel never took the advice seriously.)

Clifton Fadiman died in 1999, leaving Barzun, alone of my three musketeers, to persist into the next century. My son, a lawyer with access to Lexis-Nexus, retrieved for me many of Fadiman's obituaries. I learned that he had assembled over two dozen anthologies deal-

---

*I learned, alas, from her essay in the winter 2001 *American Scholar* that she had deserted the loft and moved to western Massachusetts.

ing with far-flung subjects, from wine to limericks to personal philosophies. I learned that his encyclopedic knowledge was utilized for
many years by the *Encyclopedia Britannica*, and that he meditated publicly
on children's literature. I was sadly reminded by the obituaries that
Dwight MacDonald had decades ago called Fadiman the "high priest
of midcult," but then the opinions of MacDonald had never engaged
me. No, it was precisely, essentially Fadiman's lack of pomposity, his
wish to be read by the intelligent, the curious, the serious, the un-
ponderous that had first attracted me to him, and it was precisely these
sorts of individuals to whom he appealed throughout his life. I learned
that he, like Mark Van Doren, had been a book reviewer for the *Nation*.
I was reminded of how, in his *New Yorker* columns, he had regrettably
mocked Gertrude Stein and William Faulkner, but I understood that
his passion for clarity and his honesty must, upon occasion, lead to
some offense. In claiming him as my model, I granted his assessment
that if only pedants read you, you cut no swath in the world. He loved
puzzles, puns, abstruse words—I am moronic at all three—but he
liked prose to be precise, elegant, and unequivocal, while at the same
time seeking a wide audience.

The women's movement rescued me from the need to abjure an academic career—as the change in academic attitudes toward Jewishness
had not arrived in time for Fadiman—and I did not in the end try to
pursue the career of reviewer he had so estimably modeled for me.
Without an academic position, he gracefully transformed popular reviewing into an art and managed, after a poor boyhood in Brooklyn
and a Columbia College education with Trilling and Barzun as fellow
students, to enjoy as innocently as possible the good things of life. He
may have called himself, with excessive modesty, a sieve, but he was
the best sieve we have ever had.

FADIMAN ON WOMEN

When I think of the best reviews I have read
in the last twenty years, two come quickly to mind. One is a
whopper of a job by Laurence Stallings in the Sun of perhaps
twelve years ago. It performed several major operations on the
autobiography of Emma Goldman, as a result of which the
patient expired. It was cruel, but it was superb.

CLIFTON FADIMAN, Reading I've Liked

———

IT WAS SURELY A SIGN of the times that, when I first read and enjoyed *Reading I've Liked* in 1941, it did not occur to me that Fadiman
was particularly hard on women, though the phrase "hard on women"
certainly requires some amplification. Apart from all the obvious con-
notations and meanings of the phrase, I mean it in a sense best ex-
pounded by Simone de Beauvoir (and one hates to imagine what Fadiman would have thought of *her*). Above all Beauvoir tried to analyze
a woman's situation in the world: what a woman does or says is not
always expressive of the woman in her, yet whatever a woman does or
says is done by a woman. The aim of feminism is to free women from
having either to eliminate their sexual subjectivity or to find themselves imprisoned by it.* Fadiman clearly considered all women, simply because they belonged to the female sex, to be imprisoned and
unable to reach beyond it—least of all when they wrote books.

These views of Fadiman's on women would never change; they are
already evident in *Reading I've Liked*. I blush to admit that at fifteen
I identified with his harsh remarks about "women readers" and the
books intended for them. Fadiman described these women readers

*This description of Beauvoir's philosophy is taken almost word for word from Toril
Moi, *What Is a Woman and Other Essays*. Moi's book is the clearest and most cogent analysis
available of that much misread text, *The Second Sex*.

as descended from the Victorian female reader for whom, Fadiman wrote, "novel reading was a disease," was, in fact, a form of daydreaming. "For her, reading became a drug, a kind of literary marijuana, an instrumentality for the production of needed visions." This was not only true—Florence Nightingale had said so, but who knew that in 1941?—it confirmed me in my jejune refusal to identify myself as a "woman." I wanted to be a "Fadiman," sex unnecessary to the definition. Neither a Victorian woman nor one of Fadiman's despised commuters' wives, I happily shared his scorn.

To this dismissal of women readers Fadiman added the dismissal of women characters. Picking the ten books he thought would still be alive and read in five hundred years, only one was by a woman (*Little Women*) and was included no doubt in the interests of what we would today call diversity. Having included it, Fadiman did not mention it again. But he pondered on his other selections, noting that three of his titles — *Moby Dick*, *Robinson Crusoe*, and *Treasure Island* — "have no women characters to speak of." He did however, and balm it was to my youthful heart, pick *Alice in Wonderland* "as the one book likely to outlast the nine others." Of his ten choices, several were children's books all, apart from *Alice*, with boy heroes. (Today, I note in a published interview with the author of the fabulously successful Harry Potter books, that while the hero, Harry, is a boy, the author's favorite character is a girl named Hermione. We do move on, if slowly.)

Reading I've Liked offers the first of a multitude of instances in which Fadiman, reaching for an example of a not-to-be-admired book, always, always picked one by a woman. Clearly his definition of a bad book came close to being a book of female authorship. Thus, discussing his reviewing for the *New Yorker*, he avers: "There is no such animal as a typical *New Yorker* reader, but we know that most of this magazine's readers do not enjoy Temple Bailey," a popular woman author of the time. Similarly, in answering what a reviewer is to do when "confronted with a book by a close friend," he mockingly asserts that he chooses as friends "only those who write well." But he feels compelled to add: "I do not know what would happen in the event that I should get to conceive a warm personal affection for, let us say, Miss Gertrude

Stein. However, careful planning should enable me to head off this possibility."

Let us follow Fadiman on his misogynist path through his later works, which I did not read at the time of publication and have only now perused, with a certain amazement at his meanness, always directed at women. I also am dismayed by my own willingness, unforgivable even in a teenaged reader of *Reading I've Liked*, gladly to accept these views of women.

Party of One, appearing in 1955, included the following gems indicating that his bias, unlike mine, did not change with the years: "It is notable that the doctrine of the omnipotence of love has often been proclaimed by the most sorry-looking females, such as George Sand, Mme. de Staël, and Elizabeth Barrett Browning." One cannot but wonder if he had read any of the three women lately. Even by 1955, before many of the major biographies of these women had appeared, his remarks were startlingly inappropriate. (In a later section, the reader will encounter Barzun's encomium to the great Mme. de Staël.)

Referring to Virginia Woolf's essay "Mr. Bennett and Mrs. Brown," Fadiman quips: "Such novels, she said, seemed to call for action on your part: reform the economic system, improve education, divorce your wife. I think Virginia Woolf thought up this pretty theory to camouflage the fact that she just didn't like novels so different from her own." My point here is that this sort of snide remark is never, in all of Fadiman I have read, directed against a male writer, not even Faulkner whom Fadiman reviled in a long review for the *New Yorker*. Magically, when he reaches for a sorry example of writing, behold, it is a woman writer he finds at his fingertips. Remarking yet again on the readers of his *New Yorker* reviews, he tells us that "most of the magazine's readers did not enjoy, let us say, Frances Parkinson Keyes." Sometimes his aspersions seem strange indeed: noting that *Lolita* is banned in Australia and France, he adds: "Over here it's virtually required reading in the women's clubs." What women's clubs could these possibly be? But no chance to insult women can be let go by.

As we move on to his second collection, *Any Number Can Play*, 1957, odd ideas about women—and particularly odd from so urbane and intelligent a man—continue: "Probably [women's] tendency to express things in terms of personal reminiscence flows from the greater concreteness of the female imagination. Joan of Arc was one of the very few women who lived and died for an abstract idea, and I have always been a little uneasy about the absoluteness of her femininity." One would hardly have dared to ask how he defined "femininity."

George Eliot, Fadiman believes, "still remains less a popular favorite than the special darling of a few influential critics such as F. R. Leavis." One can hardly blame Fadiman for calling Leavis an influential critic—he was frighteningly influential, even upon Lionel Trilling—but why pick George Eliot's work as an example of unread classics? Did he believe her less read than Melville or Defoe?

Since I have mentioned George Eliot, it is perhaps useful in this connection to compare Henry James's comments on her to Fadiman's. It is to be remembered that Fadiman admired James this side idolatry, but not, it seems, in writing about women. Here is James on George Eliot's looks, offering a model it never occurred to Fadiman, despite his admiration for James, to emulate:

> To begin with she is magnificently ugly—deliciously hideous. She has a low forehead, a dull grey eye, a vast pendulous nose, a huge mouth, full of uneven teeth. . . . Now in this vast ugliness resides a most powerful beauty which, in a very few minutes steals forth and charms the mind, so that you end as I ended, in falling in love with her. Yes, behold me literally in love with this great horse-faced blue-stocking. I don't know in what the charm lies, but it is thoroughly potent. . . . Altogether she has a larger circumference than any woman I have ever seen.

It might be argued that James knew George Eliot and Fadiman did not. For Dorothy Canfield Fisher, however, one woman he did know and, indeed, met with regularly on the board of the Book-of-the-Month Club, he had only patronizing, if kind, praise: "She has the freshest eye and the warmest heart of all of us. I think she tended to like books in which good came out triumphant; she was herself a lay saint and a book that made an appeal to the heart and to morality made a great appeal to her, though perhaps these books weren't always the best books of the month." This mildly disdainful sentence, posing as compliment, would be hard to match. Meanwhile, as quoted in Janice Radway, he praised his male colleague Henry Canby as "a scholar with the widest human sympathies, not a scholar of the study only." And not, of course, a saint: men do not aspire to sainthood.

Willa Cather, in a similar fashion, is offered casual praise: she will be preserved "by the grace of her style and the exactness of her sensibility"; no deeper literary virtues will sustain her reputation. Between contempt and faint praise, was there no woman he believed worthy of unmitigated commendation? There were, as far as I can tell, two: Emily Dickinson and Madame Curie. The essay on Madame Curie is in *Party of One*, and is wholly complimentary.

Enter Conversing, the 1962 collection of *Holiday* essays, affords little comfort to a feminist heart. When he condemns "the quasi-religion of Togetherness," he finds his examples in Jean Kerr and Shirley Jackson, "whose... pictures of family life would drive a reflective young man to sterilization." Had he never read "The Lottery," Jackson's now classic story about stoning a wife and family woman to death? In essay after essay, the example he reaches for to illustrate some negative point is inevitably female. When he is trying to define a "celebrity," therefore, "it might prove a slippery task to pin down the precise accomplishment of an Elsa Maxwell." No male example is offered. Lest we miss the point, we learn that Churchill is not a celebrity "in the sense that, say, Barbara Hutton is one." After discussing the relative values of contemporary books by men, we are informed that "*Peyton Place* is laborious trash." No male writers are dismissed in so summary a fashion. And today, in this new century, in A. O. Scott's review of a Mary McCarthy biography, Fadiman is quoted as having dubbed McCarthy's fiction "high-grade back-fence gossip." Hardly an admirer of Mary McCarthy or her works, I am nonetheless stunned at the asperity of this judgment from a usually—if the author is male—genial book reviewer.

What, as Trilling might say (though surely in another connection) are "we" to make of this? I have several purposes: first, to indicate how beyond anyone's notice, let alone objection, was this sort of unthinking misogyny through the 1940s, '50s, and most of the '60s; second, to recognize how readily I condoned it as a young woman, how I failed to notice it even as a graduate student, and how bizarre it seems to me now.

Third, and most important, I find this careless, casual cruelty in Fadiman significant because it marks so clearly the best sort of person I could choose, from those in the public, nonacademic sphere, as a model, as the personification of what I hoped to become. Not only was there a complete lack of any female model—because Fadiman was right, women were mostly extolling what he called "togetherness" and what we now identify as "family values"—but, like any outcast hoping to join the inner circle, I was willing to condemn those with whom I did not wish to be identified, even though they were "my" people. In choosing these three male models, I not only ignored their lack of respect for women, I applauded it. I was the literary Phyllis Schlafly of my time, except that she tells women to stay home while she herself works, and I, more honestly, worked while telling women to get out of the home—something few of them in those years seemed to want to do.

One wonders, without daring to speculate, why Fadiman was so casually misogynist. Trilling's conception of women differed from Fadiman's: Trilling's male-centeredness was strangely powerful and, to some extent, frightening. Certainly in this as in much else, he was dominated by Freudian ideas; perhaps it is truer to say that Freud's view of women met an easy welcome in Trilling's mind. (Trilling's quite astonishing, and not altogether conscious, resistance to any possible claim women might have upon his critical intelligence deserves a chapter of its own—which it will get.) As for Barzun, he was, as far as I could judge, the least driven by fear of female accomplishment; indeed, he consented to become my friend.

Veracity forces me to acknowledge that Fadiman's sweeping dismissals of women writers did not have the force or the resonance of the other two men's opinions. This was no doubt due to the fact that he was, in the end, "only a reviewer," whose words were hardly remembered in detail from one review to the next. He had been a glittering model for me in my youth; by the time literary criticism had become my profession, the calling of reviewer sparkled less alluringly in my dreams. Or perhaps it was only that the model of a misogynous reviewer failed any longer to appeal, and my energies were needed to cope with the misogyny of my two seminar professors. For all that, I remember him and his early books with lasting pleasure and affection.

LIONEL TRILLING

[Edmund Wilson and I] made no connection whatever.
Nor, indeed, did we ever become at all well acquainted
after other meetings during the years, but I speak of Wilson
in a personal way because he had so personal an effect
upon me. He seemed, in his own person . . . to propose
and to realize the idea of the literary life.

LIONEL TRILLING, A Gathering of Fugitives

EXACTLY SO MIGHT I have spoken of Lionel Trilling. Except that, for me, Trilling proposed not only the idea of the literary life but, odd as it must seem, the possibility of a literary life for women. Not at first: certainly not. At first he was simply the teacher who, as I wrote in 1979, quoting William Gibson, laid a finger on my soul. What a pompous, blush-making phrase: yet it perfectly describes what he did, although the word "soul" is no longer the one we would choose. But what other can I offer?

Before it occurred to me that he might be a guide to the reading and writing of literature as a feminist undertaking, he provided me with exactly the words for the conflict central to myself at that time. This was the conflict between the comforts of what I thought of as my bourgeois background and the growing conviction that not to relinquish those comforts was to betray the ideals I had come to esteem. I had begun by wishing to shed everything that spoke only of status, or taste, or upper middle class expectations. My parents' rise to the middle class had made such objects essential to them. My father drove a Cadillac, which I thought bespoke all that I was struggling to rid myself of—not that I refused frequently to borrow it, always with guilty distaste. I well remember being invited to a faculty apartment when I was part of a Columbia seminar in the 1950s; I thought it altogether the most appealing home I had ever visited. The furniture appeared to have been accumulated, rather than carefully selected; there was a comfortable, casual air about it all. Back then, I knew no apartment of my parents' generation that did not shout, "Look how carefully contrived I am," looking, indeed, as though the decorator had left five minutes ago. (It was of course my horror of "bourgeois" standards that, blessedly, kept me from the suburbs, a life that, in the 1960s, would quite literally have destroyed me.)

At the same time, like Trilling, I deeply valued various aspects of the society I had grown up in—certain manners, courtesy, generosity, the opportunity for a good education, and the assurance of a better life for one's children than one's parents had enjoyed—not to mention the convenience of bathrooms and functioning kitchens.

My profound ambivalence has changed little over fifty years, but the 1960s have intervened, so I am no longer eccentric or peculiar among my contemporaries. In 1950, when I first listened to Trilling, the struggle between the standards insisted upon by, for example, the women in my class at Wellesley and those I instinctively honored was very troubling indeed. Unimportant as I now regard it, I can nonetheless remember the daily refusal to become what so many of my peers had become. And Trilling understood that daily discord, not of course in the terms in which I have described it, but in its essence. He was, in his essay "The Princess Casamassima," inviting each of us "to put *his* own motive under examination, suggesting that reality is not as *his* conventional education has led him to see it" (emphasis mine). Calling it "moral realism," Trilling spoke of the "dangers of the moral life itself."

"You have no position," Richard Sennett, writing in the *New Yorker*, reports having once upbraided Trilling. "You are always in between."

"Between," responded Trilling, "is the only honest place to be."

Between was where I so disturbingly found myself; Trilling seemed to me to understand this, as Sennett has confirmed he did. Trilling was speaking of moral righteousness, urging that we work with intelligence for what we want, while aware of the dangers. As I have already suggested, he understood what Henry James's *The Princess Casamassima* taught, that we must not destroy society in general in order to change certain social forms. Trilling's interpretation of James's novel perfectly evoked the sense of being between two stools with which I struggled.

I had always believed this, and still do. Revolution yes; anarchy, no. And for me revolution meant exactly what it came to mean in the 1960s: an upheaval that threatened but did not destroy; that induced change but did not annihilate. Yet I was obviously destined in the early 1960s to embody the central conflict within emerging feminism. On the one hand was Betty Friedan, with her appeal to those very suburban women whom I had resisted joining and whose desperation I had avoided; on the other hand were the women of the fighting left, disruptive, daring, admirable, I thought, but not for me. As Trilling wrote in his essay on James's novel, "sometimes society offers an opposition of motives in which the antagonists are in such a balance of authority and appeal that a man who so wholly perceives them as to embody them in his very being cannot choose between them and is therefore destroyed. This is known as tragedy" (emphasis mine).

I am far from suggesting that the conflict I experienced then in any way reached the significance of tragedy as Trilling described it. The fact was, however, that I felt this conflict with the world about me as central to my being. As John Rodden writes of Trilling, "his work invites an intensely personal response in the reader, as one similarly engaged in the struggle of shaping a self in a skeptical modern age . . . his theme was nothing less than a style of living: the question of how to live the intellectual life." In my case, the world that had given me my education stood for something I could not accept. Compared to Hyacinth, torn between the high gifts of civilization and the suffering of the masses who did not enjoy these gifts, my own dilemma seems trivial indeed. I now know, however, that it adumbrated something close to tragedy; this would become evident when women struggled to join the academic and other fraternities. Far too many young women in the early days of feminism feared that if they demanded their way into the academy, they would somehow destroy its moral being, its fragile essence. Had feminism not succeeded in those years, many individuals would have been destroyed who naively assumed that all men who had achieved high position in the academy had done so purely from merit, never from special advantages. Trilling himself must have known this. Jews had not been excluded from Columbia's English department, or any other venue, because they could not meet its academic standards; the ban against women was similar.

Irving Howe would write in an obituary that Trilling "believed passionately—and taught a whole generation also to believe—in the power of literature, its power to transform, elevate and damage." At the time, literature's ability to damage did not resonate with me. Many years later, however, when I became the colleague of Trilling's ardent male followers, I discovered how damage might follow from such devotion, a devotion that excluded so much from its understanding of the great authors. When I first knew his teachings, Trilling, for example in quoting Keats, gave me the literary support I needed: in his essay on Keats in *The Opposing Self*, Trilling wrote that Keats "believed that life was given to him to find the right use of it, that it was a kind of continuous magical confrontation requiring to be met with the right answer." But Steven Marcus, one of the "disciples," wrote an obituary in the *New York Times Book Review* that limited Trilling to what his male students saw as his major contribution: "To those of us who read [*The Liberal Imagination*] at the time, it was unmistakable that a major figure in modern literary criticism had put in his appearance." True enough, but it was, I came to feel, Trilling's stature that his male students aspired to imitate, not the aching resolution of a social conflict. In my subsequent experience with Trilling's male followers, it seemed to me that the only conflict they experienced was in their fight against feminism and the challenge it brought to male dominance in the field of literary studies.

The powerful effect of *The Liberal Imagination* was never anywhere denied. The book was received as the amazing accomplishment it was, doing, as Dan Jacobson put it, "full justice to both the terms of its title, being truly liberal and imaginative in its insights." Jacobson, like all of us, remembers the excitement with which he read it. What followed *The Liberal Imagination*, however, struck many as somehow lacking the sense of purpose and the clarity of thought that had marked the earlier book. I remember that Trilling ceased to have the same overwhelming effect on me once I had become a professor and had moved into a life that somewhat resolved the conflict I had earlier endured. I assumed that this change was due less to him, his teachings and writings, than to my own maturation and, most of all, to the arrival of feminism.

But today, reading over a few book reviews and articles on Trilling written in the 1960s, I perceive that he had, indeed, come to a kind of stasis. Dan Jacobson puts the matter as I, though far less clearly, experienced it. "The ideological issues which had provided the occasion for *The Liberal Imagination* . . . had deserted him, had ceased to be of interest." Trilling, Jacobson observed, "could not put by his spokesman's manners, his stylistic affectations, pomposities, and indirections." Had I read that sentence in the 1960s, when my need for Trilling's guidance had lessened but my admiration was still untrammeled, I would have deeply resented those words. Reading them today, I cannot deny their pertinence: I find Jacobson quoting a passage from Trilling's essay on *Emma*, but it is not the outrageously misogynist passage I myself would have picked and indeed quote later. Here is the paragraph Jacobson picked, as he says, "quite at random":

> We cannot be slow to see what is the basis of this energy and style and intelligence. It is self-love. There is great power of charm in self-love, although, to be sure, the charm is an ambiguous one. We resent it and resist it, yet we are drawn by it, if only it goes with a little grace or creative power. Nothing is easier to pardon than the mistakes and excesses of self-love: if we are quick to condemn them, we take pleasure in forgiving them. And with good reason, for they are the extravagance of the first of the virtues, the most basic and biological of the virtues, that of self-preservation.

Jacobson remarks that "by the end of the paragraph one feels oneself to be a long, long way from *Emma* and hardly any closer to Trilling." I agree with Jacobson that we are far from Emma, a heroine whose imprisonment as a female, in no way mitigated by self-love, Trilling overlooked. But I do not agree that we are far from Trilling: indeed, we are where he was then and always in my eyes. I may debate, and did debate, what he said; I never had anything but admiration for the way he said it, at least up to the time of Jacobson's review. When *Beyond Culture* was published in 1966, Trilling had become an icon, and young critics were earning their spurs by denigrating his prose and his ideas.

In 1963 Joseph Frank published an essay entitled "Lionel Trilling and the Conservative Imagination." The shift from liberal to conservative as adjectives defining Trilling is striking and accurate. Frank wrote: "it is of the utmost importance not to confuse the boundaries of the ideal and the real, the aesthetic and the social; not to endow social passivity and quietism *as such* with the halo of aesthetic transcendence" (emphasis Frank's). Frank recognizes the greatness of Trilling's essay on *The Princess Casamassima*, but is amazed, as I was, by Trilling's admiration for Lady Bertram in *Mansfield Park*. How this somnambulant creature could speak to "our secret inexpressible hopes" bewilders Frank as it does me. Frank said there was the danger of "moral and cultural stultification" in Trilling (and, as I always thought, in Lady Bertram). But I was apparently able to forgive the egregiousness of this particular Trilling view when I first read it.

Trilling's power to persuade me had not abated, nor had my willingness to overlook those ideas I could not altogether countenance. As to what Trilling wrote in *Freud and the Crisis of Our Culture*, I remember deciding not to read this, having already determined that Trilling's views on Freud and mine were entirely incompatible. It would be many years before I could distinguish between Freud's revolutionary perceptions and his outrageous views on women—about which Diana Trilling would declare: "Nowhere in his writings does Freud express sympathy for the problems which pertain to women alone. On the contrary, his misogyny is now taken for granted even by his most admiring students." I did not then take it for granted. (I was interested to learn that, although Trilling had suffered great obstructions to his writing, he wrote *Freud and the Crisis of Our Culture* in three weeks, thus indicating, it seems, that no new process of analysis was deemed necessary.)

Trilling's refusal to take any notice of or to offer any understand-

ing, if not encouragement, to the women's movement as it flowered
in the late 1960s and early '70s certainly does significantly characterize his work during that period. I began to sense that this failure did
somehow stand in the way of his ability to achieve the moral purpose
evident in his earlier work. Perhaps I would not have allowed myself
consciously to entertain such a thought during the 1960s, but as I
later met up with the same recalcitrance in Trilling's male disciples, I
understood that, odd as it may seem, he had offered them less than he
had offered me. For they could only strive to become him, while I had
internalized the tensions he had enunciated and, greatly to his credit,
had been able to translate them into fields of endeavor he would have
despised. ("Trilling did not cultivate disciples, for he was 'a sorcerer
who took no apprentices,'" Morris Dickstein, who did not achieve
tenure at Columbia, has written. The fact probably is that Trilling did
not cultivate Dickstein; certainly he did cultivate disciples, many of
whom I taught with.)

Trilling and I encountered one another again during the uprisings
at Columbia in 1968, and later in 1970; he had left the graduate school,
where I taught, and retreated to the college for all his courses. I remember him from the 1968 faculty meetings as we all endeavored to
deal with the situation. Memories of what went on differ, and always
will,* but in the end Trilling and I interpreted the uprisings differently.
In a 1968 *Partisan Review* interview with Donadio, who was then teaching at Columbia, Trilling said that he did not believe there was any
record of "manifest injustice at Columbia in relation to students." On
the contrary, he went on, "I'll even say my sense of the Administration's attitudes, is that they have been eminently decent and humane.
Representations to the contrary seem to me to be factitious or perfec-
tionistic." Most of us, on the other hand, understood that the administration had for far too long refused any consultations with student

---

*As Stephen Donadio wrote in his account of the 1968 Columbia uprising, the press
coverage of the events pointed up "the distortions, more or less gross, which appear
in the news media daily. Few people who experienced the crisis will ever read the *New
York Times* in quite the same way again" (*Commentary*, September 1968).

groups requesting them. As Diana Trilling noted in "On the Steps of Low Library" in *We Must March My Darlings*, the administration "had never perceived the need to set up an apparatus for discourse between students and administration. They seemed unaware of the difference between the students they had addressed in the past and those they addressed today." Or, as Donadio puts it in "Black Power at Columbia," graduate students were

> dealing with the powerlessness they felt as graduate students at Columbia, expressing their disgust with the dreary "institutional" quality of the education they were receiving and about which they had never been consulted. This sense of powerlessness, when linked with the fact of Columbia's notoriously retrograde program of financial aid, accounted for the feeling of many graduate students that they were not only being ignored but taken for granted and rooked as well.

Donadio makes the point that the question of race was the overwhelming factor in the crisis: when black students took over Hamilton Hall, Columbia College's center of classrooms and administration, the uprisings reached a new stage of violence—not from the black but from the white students. Trilling does not mention this in his interview with Donadio, nor does he mention the powerful factor of resistance to the Vietnam War. Diana Trilling describes how most of the faculty, unlike Trilling himself, came to support the uprisings:

> The day after the bust, when the strike was called, far from a majority of the faculty supported it. But as the days passed and the professors began to talk to their students, fewer and fewer found it possible to make the break with them which would have been the consequence of their insisting that classes be held in the struck buildings. These newly politicized students were too genuine in their commitment to the strike, too impressive in their new gravity.

As we shall see in the later discussion of Diana Trilling, her perceptions here and in many other cases were less conservative than Lionel's, and though she never set out to contradict him in any way, her impressions of their lives and actions have, as I hope to show, a value too little perceived.

I wore a white arm band with most of the faculty, and tried to intervene between the police, who were, however understandably, angrily brutal, and the members of the Columbia community. Whatever the rights or wrongs of the 1968 uprising, and the subsequent strike in 1970 after the bombing of Cambodia and the murder of the Kent State students, Columbia would never be the same again. Whether a more intelligent administration might have steered a less violent course cannot be known. But when I came to write about the uprising in a detective novel, Poetic Justice, I more or less portrayed Trilling as an attractive if slightly flawed character. This was in the early 1970s, which certainly suggests that his hold upon my imagination had not slackened.

In an essay published in 1979 but written for a speech some years earlier, I summed up what Trilling had taught me and suggested how his insights might be applied to women, as unlikely as that might seem. I know that this speech, which I believe was delivered to an audience of Danforth fellowship recipients, was written after Trilling's death in 1975; I did not, however, feel free to speak as I did just because Trilling was dead. Had he been living, he would never, I could be certain, have known of my talk or of how I had interpreted his views.

I did not feel either guilt or uneasiness at using Trilling's words for a feminist purpose; it seemed to me a natural and even complimentary thing to do. Toril Moi recently declared that the famous phrase of Audre Lorde's, "The master's tools will never dismantle the master's house," does not make sense to her; I have myself always wondered at the phrase's wide acceptance and was glad to have confirmation from Moi. As she suggested, a sledgehammer is a sledgehammer. Like me, however innocently in the early 1970s, Moi does not see why a feminist should not read Freud, say—or Trilling—and appropriate their theories for a use they did not intend.

My suggestion to young women, then, was to "look especially to his descriptions of the quests and dreams of young men in search of a self." I quoted to them Trilling's admonishment to "Act out of your own high sense of yourself." Trilling had told young men to cultivate that aspect of themselves that has for its function the preservation of the self. At a time when many young women still saw their destiny as adequately fulfilled in volunteering—that is, the offering of the self to others for their use—this advice seemed to me essential.

Trilling had always noted the profound disinclination of Americans to confront tragedy, just as he portrayed in his novel, *The Middle of the Journey*, their distaste for any discourse about death. He believed that "we fulfill ourselves by choosing what is painful and difficult and necessary," and I urged young women to join in that "we." Enacting feminism, and a high sense of self, has never been easy or comfortable for women; it is painful and difficult, but it is also, I urged them, necessary. The question, I went on to say, is one of transformation, both of institutions and of women's consciousness.

Later, I would point to one of Trilling's most famous formulations: the "Young Man from the Provinces." In *The Liberal Imagination* Trilling describes him thus:

> He need not come from the provinces in literal fact, his social class may constitute his province. But a provincial birth and rearing suggest the simplicity and the high hopes he begins with—he starts with a great demand upon life and a great wonder about its complexity and promise. He may be of good family but he must be poor. He is intelligent, or at least aware, but not at all shrewd in worldly matters. He must have acquired a certain amount of education, should have learned something about life from books, although not the truth.

Not all young men are "young men from the provinces"; neither are all young women. But there are more such women today than there used to be; today, at least, women are likely to start "with a great demand upon life," and their sex, of course, constitutes their province. When, as a new graduate student, I heard Trilling lecture, I knew I was a "young man from the provinces," just as I knew I wished to join the male professorial fraternity—even as I also knew I was neither one of Trilling's young men nor likely to achieve the high hopes I began with.

While the conflict between my gender and my hopes never released its grip on me, the friction inherent in being a Jew at Columbia or anywhere else entirely escaped me. I knew of anti-Semitism; it was impossible not to know of it; the concentration camps had hardly escaped our attention; perhaps we thought that the gentile world, in shame, would try to make it up to us. I don't remember contemplating the subject at all in those years. The wish I and my family had long held, to disappear quietly into the gentile world, to assimilate entirely, had become untenable but not less attractive. It would be many years before claiming my Jewishness was an effortless task. Perhaps this is why, as I have suggested, I never thought of Trilling—or earlier, of Fadiman—in this connection. While I "identified" with Trilling in all his literary and social judgments, nothing in my life compared to his early experiences as a Jew. By the time I read "Wordsworth and the Rabbis," I was actually startled to find him discussing the Jewish training in his boyhood, and that essay was only published in 1955.* (This declaration of his training for his bar mitzvah did not astonish me, however, quite as much as my recent discovery that his first published essay, in 1924, had been on Emily Brontë's poetry; Jane Austen and Edith Wharton apart, he would not write an academic article on another woman.) I always, without much thought, considered Trilling English—not literally so, but English all the same. His name, Lionel, his profound concern with British literature, his general English-gentlemanly demeanor. Much later I learned that his mother had been born in En-

---

*Rereading "Wordsworth and the Rabbis" now (in *The Opposing Self*), I am reminded how profoundly I disagreed with Trilling at that time about the glories of the ordinary life. He castigated T. S. Eliot for denigrating in *The Cocktail Party* the ordinary, unheroic life. I was wholly on Eliot's side, and still am. But nothing in those days could have pried me from my Trilling admiration, and indeed nothing did for many years.

gland and had hoped he would go to Oxford. Something of all this, entwined with my own ardent anglophilia, assigned him to England.

As I came to reconsider Trilling in the present day, I made the startling discovery that his stance in regard to his Jewishness—always allowing for the differences in historical circumstances—was exactly the one I have today slowly, reluctantly, inevitably adopted. Morris Dickstein reports, in his foreword to Rodden's collection *Lionel Trilling and the Critics*, that Trilling had written in 1944, in the *Contemporary Jewish Record*: "I do not think of myself as a 'Jewish writer.' I do not have it in mind to serve by my writing any Jewish purpose. I would resent it if a critic of my work were to discover in it either faults or virtues which he called Jewish." Trilling did recognize—and his honesty here, as always, still moves me—that saying this at this time showed "a certain gracelessness—if only because millions of Jews are suffering simply because they have the heritage that I so minimize in my own intellectual life." Dickstein concedes that "Trilling could hardly acknowledge what was happening to the Jews of Europe in 1944." Trilling's ability to take in this horror, like mine and that of so many others then, was to be delayed by several years. The timing of this statement was, to say the least, regrettable; for him then, as for me then and now, the sentiment was honest.

In "Young in the Thirties" (1966), Trilling wrote: "The situation of the American Jew has changed so much [since the 1930s] that it may be hard for some to understand the need for such efforts"—those efforts being for the Jew to claim "his" Jewish identity, not through religion or Zionism, but through his sense of authenticity as a Jew. ("Authenticity" was one of Trilling's magic words, canonized in his Harvard lectures of 1970, entitled *Sincerity and Authenticity*.) ★

What I find particularly compelling in Trilling's account of his struggles as a Jew is that, as a young man, he found anti-Semitism an advantage, enabling him and his Jewish confreres to define them-

---

★ In a footnote to his 1966 article, Trilling notes that the English TLS has adopted Yiddishisms.

selves against the society that shunned them. As he wrote, "It helped give life the look of reality." He recalled that in his college days he searched, as all college students do, for some social entity in which he might believe, which might help to define him to himself. That he welcomed his Jewishness in that light—as I now discover he did—explains so much about him: his continuing sense of himself as involved in the most serious of searches, on his own behalf and on behalf of literature, and the genuine impression he gave of always thinking, always plumbing the depths. Above all, it emphasizes what to me appears even now as his courage never, even in those bad old days, to deny his Jewishness. One of his many rewards for his integrity was the many students, Jewish as well as non-Jewish, who followed him, sensing how honorable he was in that and other ways. The names of these students suggest the power of his influence: Fritz Stern, John Hollander, Jason Epstein, Richard Howard, Steven Marcus, Norman Podhoretz, Louis Simpson, Byron Dobell, Robert Gottlieb, Robert Shulman, Joseph Kraft, and there are more. As Diana Trilling would describe it in *The Beginning of the Journey,*

> At all stages of education there are teachers who become symbolical figures for their student—they have it in common with analysts that certain of their students vest their phantasies in them. While Lionel himself never proposed that literary criticism was an instrument of power and prestige, his work implicitly suggested a significant public role for the teacher-critic. . . . Lionel represented for his gifted students a literary academic whose thought ranged well beyond the academy, linking literature to the wider political and moral life of the nation. The social relevance and moral intensity which in our American mid-century gave criticism its newly important role in society made Lionel himself into a kind of moral exemplar for his students, someone whose life and character might set the pattern for their own public and private choices.

I was not one of them; they were, of course, all men. But I had to deny Trilling's Jewishness as well to myself to worship him as I did.

My sense of Jewishness as granting me a meaningful relationship to society arrived very late in my life; earlier, I could perceive no advantages to the condition. I was certainly seeking for a social entity, but it was not as a Jew but as a woman.

By the time I spoke in the Danforth lecture about Trilling's pertinence to the condition of women, I had already accepted the idea that my dialogue with him did not require his presence; indeed, his presence would have inhibited it. For by 1972 I had lost any idea that the Trilling of that time could mean much to me or to my hopes for change in the conditions of women. In any case, by 1972 Trilling seemed to have accepted the presence of women in the academic world, if not in his particular enclave, and was now troubled by affirmative action.

Trilling's 1972 Jefferson Lecture in the Humanities, *Mind in the Modern World*, spoke of the failure of mind in the contemporary academic world. The mind, in the academic profession and elsewhere, had, he said, borrowing the phrase from H. G. Wells, "come to the end of its tether." From implications and references, Trilling made clear that the efforts of the left to enlarge the opportunities for minorities were, if not responsible for, symptomatic of the failure of mind he saw all about him. It was no longer women who threatened his "old thing of a man's college"; indeed, in the published version of his lecture, he was forced to change the wording of his remarks:

> The affirmative action program, as it is called, applies not only to certain ethnic groups but also to women. In the text of my lecture as it was delivered, the latter stipulation was included in my paraphrase of the program's directive. I omit it here because what I go on to say about the effect of the program on academic standards does not bear immediately upon it. At the present time the number of trained academic women is perhaps large enough to support the frequently expressed belief that no lowering of academic standards can result from the requirement that women be proportionately represented on faculties. Doubtless it will eventually be possible to say the same thing of the disadvantaged groups, the sooner the better. When that time comes,

the anomaly of prescribed social or sexual representation in the
life of the mind will perhaps seem necessary to no one.

I found, and still find, this statement so astounding that I hardly know
how to deal with it, except to pretend amusement at the two "perhaps," particularly the first, and the implication that women are "pro-
portionately" represented on faculties. For Trilling, nothing, no social adjustment, no sacrifice for future benefit, could weigh against
the loss of the male-centered academic community into which he had
fought his way, and which he had for so long protected from intrusion.
That was, during his lifetime, the end of my unqualified admiration
for Trilling. But the very day of his death would present me with a truly
ironic end to our long, one-sided relationship.

Trilling had given his books to the Columbia Library, and had
agreed to address the Friends of the Columbia Library, a prestigious
and financially generous group. Trilling was by now too ill to give the
address, and we heard that he had not been told of his cancer, something I found horrifying in itself. Because of this, no other speaker
could be engaged for the address, lest Trilling hear of it. I was the one
asked to replace him. Testily, I asked why none of his male "disciples"
could stand in; no reason was offered, though their overwhelming
grief was implied. In the end, I agreed to perform the task. Trilling,
as I had dreaded, died on the very day of the scheduled address. I shall
always be grateful to Gordon Ray, then head of the Guggenheim Foun-
dation, for transforming the audience from remorse to mild acceptance of me. Of course, I talked of women, ending with a quotation
from Trilling that could be interpreted as a chance for a new dispen-
sation for women.

Looking back now, I am troubled to find how little appeal Trilling
has for me today. When I consider the importance of his place in my
life, an importance in no way lessened by his ignorance of it, I regret
that in now looking over his long-pondered essays, I do not find them
particularly useful or appealing. It might be said of me that I had used
them up and was now throwing them out. But neither Fadiman nor

Barzun, as I review their writings, affects me in that way. Although Fadiman ceased persuading me in any profound way many years ago, my bemused affection for him, his love of cheese and wine, his adoration for the *Encyclopedia Britannica*, has not abated. Nor has the memory of what he taught me about writing for an intelligent public vanished. Barzun I shall write of at greater length in another chapter; suffice it to say here that my admiration for him and his writings has increased, almost in proportion to my disenchantment with Trilling.

And why my disenchantment with Trilling? It arises mainly from his tone, his almost arrogant assumption of speaking the truth as he reports what "we" think. Two examples from *A Gathering of Fugitives* will suffice: "No one, I think, is any longer under any illusion about Dickens. It is now clear that he is one of the two greatest novelists of England, Jane Austen being the other." And: "We all believe that we know all about Zola, whether we have read him or not. . . . But he has not for many years commanded our real interest, precisely, I suppose, because we believe we have him so thoroughly taped." David Brooks, writing in *Bobos in Paradise*, notices how strange and unfamiliar the intellectual landscape of the 1950s seems today. Those intellectuals, Brooks finds, "adopted prose styles that, while clear and elegant, were also portentous." Nor, he notices, were they "shy on the subject of their own importance."

As I relish the friendships that feminism has brought me, I am troubled to read in *A Gathering of Fugitives* that Trilling believed Henry Adams to have been "the last man, or perhaps the last American, to have had actual friendships. He mistrusted much in the world, but he trusted his friends, and he so far developed his great civilized talent for connection that he could be in lively communicative relationship even with his family, and even with women."

While Trilling could not, it seems, be in "lively communicative relationship even with women," one wonders why his friendship with Barzun did not strike Trilling as "actual." Barzun, in "Remembering Lionel Trilling," certainly suggests the quality of the two men's rapport; in fact, what Mark Krupnick has called "Trilling's main link to the general culture in the fifties" was his involvement, with Barzun and W. H. Auden, in two book clubs, the Reader's Subscription from 1952 to 1959, and the Mid-Century Book Club from 1959 to 1962. Neither book club succeeded financially, but surely that attempt to influence or reach a large public, undertaken with Barzun, suggests the kind of friendship Henry Adams would have enjoyed.

But so companionable an association with Trilling was not for me. Trilling noted that the last sentence of Freud's last book "is a sentence from Goethe: 'What you have inherited from your fathers, truly possess it so as to make it your own.'" He and Freud, needless to say, spoke only to men. But if Trilling was my intellectual father, I have so far made what he taught me my own that he seems, for me although perhaps not for his male "disciples," to have quite faded away. That is surely what fathers should do.

In 1999, John Rodden published *Lionel Trilling and the Critics: Opposing Selves*, a collection of seventy articles and reviews written throughout Trilling's career. That only four of the pieces reprinted here are by women, one of them Diana Trilling, is not surprising, given the history of Trilling's generation. (When *American Scholar* published remembrances of Alfred Kazin on the occasion of his death, Kazin's wife was the only woman included.) What is, however, sharply indicative is that, of the other three pieces by women, one is Edna O'Brien's acerbic English review of Trilling's *E. M. Forster*, and the others are by an American neoconservative, Gertrude Himmelfarb, and an English Thatcherite, Shirley Robin Letwin. Himmelfarb foretells the degree to which Trilling will be embraced, from his death to the end of the century, by those who view him as a convert to, or forefather of, their reactionary views. When Diana Trilling asserts that Trilling was always a liberal, that statement is treated, as her statements so often are, as simply unreliable or wrong.

It is certainly true that, politically as in so many ways, Trilling was hard to pin down; I have already noted his tendency to remain "between." Following his experience with the communism of the 1930s,

Trilling, as I believe, evolved an apparently tentative attitude toward the political forces influencing his past and present students. It was this seeming ambivalence that made it possible to assert that he was the inspirer of a conservative political stance that he would, in my view, have refuted.

The year 2000, and the publication of Leon Wieseltier's selected essays of Lionel Trilling, *The Moral Obligation To Be Intelligent*, inspired reviews and articles, many of them by conservatives claiming Trilling as the father of neoconservatism. One of the chief marks of neoconservatism, certainly of the women promulgating its ideals, is a virulent antifeminism. Inevitably, therefore, the *New Yorker* chose Cynthia Ozick to write an extended article on Trilling, whom she, like me, remembered from when she was a graduate student. While I remember Trilling in the graduate seminar as courteous, if not encouraging to all, Ozick recalls him as "impatient; often he seemed fatigued. He had one or two favorites, whom he would praise profusely—but he was sarcastic or indifferent to others." Trilling was, to be sure, mildly scornful of women; this seems to have resonated more personally with Ozick than with me.

Ozick exceeds all others in her meanness, even cruelty, to Diana and the Trillings' son, James, accusing them both of tending "to undermine Trilling's public standing from a private vantage. Inevitably, the malicious dust of a colossus pulled down fills the nostrils." Her diatribe against Diana arises from Diana's claim to having helped Lionel to strengthen his writing. Such help is often needed by highly gifted people, nor does Diana claim to write better than Lionel, only to have suggested the sort of alterations every committed writer welcomes; in Lionel's case, these alterations could have been offered by no one else. But few stones that can be hurled at Diana Trilling remain unslung.

Six years before Ozick's *New Yorker* article, Gertrude Himmelfarb, the wife of Irving Kristol—and the mother of William Kristol, who ran Dan Quayle's campaign to become vice-president—had dedicated *On Looking into the Abyss: Untimely Thoughts on Culture and Society* "to the memory of Lionel Trilling." Himmelfarb explained that "the spirit of

Lionel Trilling hovers over the book as a whole."* Diana Trilling had been quite specific in refuting this claim. During an interview with John Rodden, she told him that an "abyss would separate the present-day political viewpoint of Lionel Trilling from that of Himmelfarb and Kristol." Diana went on to lament "the Kristols' embrace of a neo-conservative 'politics of self-interest'" and to express her "enduring regret that our political disagreement has all but ended the relationship" with her. She added that "Lionel did not live long enough to witness the rise of the neoconservative movement, but I have little question that if he had been alive and working in the eighties, he would have been highly critical of this swing to the right by our old friends." In this, as in so much else, Diana's judgments were disregarded.

I suspect that Trilling's refusal to recognize or even acknowledge the rise of feminism did much to encourage neoconservatives in their belief that he was politically on their side. Here is Himmelfarb indulging in an imaginary account of the effect of feminism on literary studies in universities: "an obscure woman writer (obscure for good literary reasons) [is] as meritorious as George Eliot who is suspect not only because she assumed that male pseudonym but because she made a profession of being a writer rather than a feminist writer." Since George Eliot is prominently admired and discussed in feminist studies in the academy, one can only suppose that Himmelfarb had never bothered to peruse even one of the many books on Victorian novelists by a feminist.

She continues: "Cleanth Brooks, Robert Penn Warren [editors of *Southern Review*] were dismayed to discover that their successors, determined to open the 'canon' to women and black writers, have little concern with the literary merit of their books." She adds that this mysterious "they" would rather teach Superman than Shakespeare. Since at Columbia Superman was taught by Professor George Stade, one of Trilling's most ardent followers, and never by any standard femi-

*This Himmelfarb essay can be found, where I found it, in John Rodden's *Lionel Trilling and the Critics*. Rodden's book is invaluable to anyone interested in Trilling.

nist, one wonders how thorough is Himmelfarb's much celebrated scholarship.

John Krupnick suggests that what preceded these recent neo-conservative claims was the sense of disappointment with the Trilling of the 1960s:

> Certainly it is reasonable to have been disappointed with Trilling in the late 1960s. But the disappointment might just as well have focused on his failure to oppose the Vietnam War rather than his failure to oppose the war's opponents. Writers on both the left and the right had reason to feel let down by Trilling. His remoteness saved him from the polemical excesses of intellectuals more deeply involved in the cultural debates of those years. But Trilling's coolness was purchased at too high a price. It now appears that Trilling's disengagement may have had less to do with a cowardly concern to protect his reputation than with a sense of bafflement.

Not that Trilling's disciple Steven Marcus, writing in the *New York Times* in 1976, found anything disappointing or disengaged in Trilling's response to the 1960s: "As he considered some of the more bizarre lunacies of the New Left or wilder manifestations of the counter-culture, he thought he saw in these rapidly fluctuating formations genuine threats to the cultural order that he affirmed, albeit minimally and with a cold, skeptical eye. He tended on the whole to see tragedy in such developments, while others tended to see farce." Marcus's interpretation of Trilling's response to the uprisings at Columbia can be seen to provide neoconservatism with the opportunity to claim Trilling as one of its own. As Ozick would put it, "By the nineteen-seventies, no question remained that was forbidden in polite society, and no answer, either; there was little left of the concept of polite society altogether. . . . The Cossacks were astride the politics of culture." Some Columbia professors, such as the conservative Daniel Bell, withdrew in horror from Columbia and fled to Harvard. The fact that there were those who had had no voice in the "polite society" here mourned carries no weight with Ozick. It is apparently on these grounds that Trilling was hailed by a group whose courtesy or practice of "polite society" is certainly not evident to those with whom they disagree.

★   ★   ★

And so the *New York Times*, on September 16, 2000, discloses, with portraits arranged chronologically, the "Faces of Neoconservatism"; Trilling, described as the "forebear," leads all the rest. Included in this group are David Brooks, whom we have seen disdaining Trilling, and George W. Bush (!), among eleven others ranging from Irving Kristol through William Bennett and Jeane Kirkpatrick. They are certainly neoconservatives all, but what Trilling is doing as the forebear is puzzling indeed. Without question, his refusal to take clear positions on political issues, his willingness to speak against affirmative action, and his refusal to recognize the claims of women, marked him, to those hungry for such evidence, as a reactionary.

I am particularly saddened by the realization that it was his appreciation for certain admirable qualities of bourgeois life—or "polite society," if that is what we must now call it—that has thrust him posthumously into this group of people. For, unlike them, he was able, as I strove to be able under his example, to mourn the price of spreading social opportunities and liberal beliefs—even as one knew the price to be not only inevitable, but paid in a worthy cause. The ability to perceive this conflict, and express it so forcibly, seems to have led to regrettable, and I believe mistaken, assumptions about Trilling's political views.

At the republication of many of his articles, then, we are reminded of him, and rightly honor his place in literary history. True, those in graduate schools today do not ponder him, yet a rejection or ignorance of earlier thought marks this current graduate generation, as it has marked them all. His direct disciples, also misreading him, have, in the view of many, propelled Columbia's English department into the disarray from which it currently suffers. Divided along political lines, the department has sadly ceased to operate as a unified example of academic accomplishment. Feminism, along with those who passionately oppose it, has been a large factor in this dissolution.

Because Trilling could balance gains and losses without disregarding either, because he was not convinced of the magnitude of his own achievements, because he knew that the keenest expressions of morality and honor are in literature—for all these reasons he will remain perhaps the best exemplar left to us, in the academic world and in the culture beyond it, of the literary mind and the literary consciousness.

TRILLING'S NOVEL

I had no doubt that my story was a serious one,
but I nevertheless wanted it to move on light feet.
LIONEL TRILLING, 1975 *introduction to*
The Middle of the Journey

ALTHOUGH TRILLING published several stories, only one novel of his, *The Middle of the Journey*, reached publication. It was written in 1947, ten years after the completion of his dissertation on Matthew Arnold, and both works were concluded with the same dramatic collapse into fatigue. On both occasions, upon finishing work on the manuscripts, he fell into a sleep of total exhaustion from which he could not be awakened. Matthew Arnold had occupied him for a dozen years, *The Middle of the Journey* for the length of a sabbatical, but each represented a particular, unique effort in his professional life. He wrote the novel in secret; even his wife knew nothing of it until it was complete. Such a secret endeavor, full of hope and the dread of failure, is not uncommon among those who have not considered themselves, nor been considered, writers of extended works of fiction.

Trilling seems always to have had dreams of being a novelist. As John Rodden reports,

> In an interview Trilling made clear that he intended to move beyond his chief identity of literary critic. Trilling said that he wished to be identified thenceforth as a novelist and reported that "from now on I plan to give a good deal of time to [writing fiction.] I'm writing a second novel at the moment." He apparently never completed the novel, and no part of it has ever been

published. (Viking's dust jacket for *The Opposing Self* had also announced the "good news" that the author of *The Middle of the Journey* was "at work on a new novel.")

The Middle of the Journey was, however, harshly reviewed by Robert Warshaw in 1947 in *Commentary*; Warshaw accused Trilling of being "unable to hold to his experience," that is, honestly to represent his own struggles in the novel. Damningly, Warshaw added: "The point is not that Mr. Trilling is not a great novelist; a healthy culture has room for the minor talent. What is significant is that Mr. Trilling has not yet solved the problem of being a novelist at all." Some have even surmised that this review so deeply wounded Trilling that he stopped writing fiction altogether.

This surmise may be a bit too dramatic: Trilling was not alone in finding the transition from critic to novelist full of psychological impediments. It is likely that no one whose life is devoted to the teaching of great fiction fails to dream of writing his or her own novel. Few do so, and those who undertake the task more often than not write detective fiction, admitting the improbability of their achieving anything comparable to the works they propound in class. Clearly, Trilling had higher hopes for his fiction than most. Yet the energy required for that one venture into fiction may well exhaust the possibility of another such effort; examples of academics who have written one novel abound.

The Middle of the Journey—the title is from the opening of Dante's *Divine Comedy*: "In the middle of the journey of our life I came to myself within a dark wood where the straight way was lost"—recounts the story of John Laskell's close encounter with death from scarlet fever. Having recovered, he travels to Connecticut to recuperate as a guest in the summer home of his friends Nancy and Arthur Croom. He is joined on the train by Gifford Maxim, who has deserted his secret communist group and is in fear of being assassinated by them. After his many years underground, Maxim is certain that they will kill him unless he protects himself by making his reappearance above ground widely known. Trilling tells us, in his introduction to the 1975 re-issue of the novel, that the character of Maxim, admittedly modeled on Whittaker Chambers, did not occur to him until he was well along in his novel.

By including Maxim, Trilling was able early in the novel to introduce the idea of death, something Laskell constantly thinks about after his recovery. After his arrival at the house of the Crooms, Laskell tries more than once to speak of his encounter with death to his friends, but they will not listen, fearing to let so distasteful an idea into their lives. Laskell becomes involved in the affairs of a local family: with the mother, to whom he makes love; with the father during a moment of masculine fishing companionship; and with the child, to whom he is affectionately drawn but for whose sudden death he feels a guilt that is neither justifiable nor without a certain validity. In the end Laskell returns to New York, having failed in his frequent attempts to speak to anyone of what most intensely concerns him: the experience of nearly dying.

There can be no question that communism and Maxim, the character modeled on Chambers, appeared to be the central facts of the novel for Trilling and for his contemporary readers. Maxim helps also to place the novel in historical time. In his introduction to the novel's reissue, Trilling speaks only of Maxim/Chambers, the Hiss-Chambers case that followed the book's original publication, and the possible reasons for the general suspicion and dislike of Chambers. In fact, as Diana Trilling points out, the book was not well received in the United States and was not sufficiently promoted by Viking, apparently because Benjamin Huebsch, head of Viking at that time, was sympathetic to communism and did not wish to support a novel he thought critical of the communist party. *The Middle of the Journey* was much more warmly received in England, and all the blurbs on the reissued volume are from English reviews. (Diana Trilling claims that Viking never served Trilling well, either then or later. All the same, if Trilling's novel was hardly greeted with the delight even some less-than-best-selling fiction enjoys, according to Diana it was still in print fifty years later.)

Communism and the character of Gifford Maxim have always been for me the least interesting aspect of what I otherwise find to be a fascinating novel, mainly, but far from entirely, because Trilling wrote it. That there is so little overlap in our ideas about communism is due almost entirely to the different generations to which we belonged. No single issue was so central as communism to Trilling's generation of intellectuals, and the issue still dominated his thought at the time he was writing *The Middle of the Journey*. My generation, however, born twenty years after his, had become concerned with communism only after the start of the cold war, and had been most passionately disturbed by the outrages perpetrated against anyone Joseph McCarthy could, reasonably or not, accuse of being a communist.

Rereading *The Middle of the Journey* now, I find a great deal of it extraordinarily interesting, and that for personal reasons as well as for admiration of the novel. The protagonist, Laskell, who clearly reflects Trilling's ideas, is neither Jewish nor married nor less than financially comfortable. Warshaw, in his *Commentary* review, was disturbed that Trilling had made his characters gentiles. Warshaw's objection seemed to rest on the "fact" that most communists were Jews (such as gentile Chambers and Hiss, for example?). The interest I take in Laskell's WASPness is hardly a historical one; it is personal. For when I came to write the first American detective novel in many years with a woman detective — stories featuring women detectives had for a time flourished but were no longer available and Agatha Christie's Miss Marple, very English and a ladylike spinster, was the only other woman detective then in print — I also gave her all the attributes that Trilling had bestowed on Laskell.

I do not suggest an influence here. *The Middle of the Journey* was published the year I graduated from college; I did not read it until I arrived at Columbia in 1951. It did not make a great impression on me — in fact I remember finding it annoying and apparently did not own or keep it, although I did own all Trilling's other works. (I recently found the novel in my bookcase; it was the 1975 reissue which I had picked up remaindered at Marboro for a dollar, as the still-attached sticker informs me.)

I remember that I discussed the novel, after first reading it, with a young man studying for his Ph.D. at Columbia—his parents and mine were friends—and informing him that I found the book too much "tell" and not enough "show." It was a ridiculous remark, which the young man properly scorned, but it amuses me to think of it now, because that foolish command not to "tell" is one repeated, so it seems, by every young editor starting out in publishing, as I did. Possibly we all take it in with mother's milk. Of course, if you are dealing with an intelligent and stimulating writer, you want tell. Movies no longer tell, which is perhaps why I find them mainly too confusing and puzzling, and without a narrative thread. Certain excellent modern novels, such as William Faulkner's, also refuse to tell; as I used to advise my students, the story will only reveal itself upon rereading. (Could this be why neither Fadiman nor Trilling cared for Faulkner?) In the case of Trilling's novel, Laskell's thoughts are the heart of the book, and its entire reason for being.

Suggesting no connection between *The Middle of the Journey* and my first detective novel in 1964, I still find it intriguing that my protagonist, Kate Fansler, was, like Trilling's Laskell, WASP, with a private income, unmarried, devoted to courtesy and the sensibility necessary for true courtesy, and greatly given to inner reflection. At the time when I wrote the first Kate Fansler novel, I was long married, had three children, was financially straitened, harried, and, then and always, Jewish. Trilling and I were certainly, as we wrote our novels, coping with quite different challenges in real life, but we let none of these challenges into our fiction. We allowed our heroes to be morally engaged, restrained in their comments, and professionally content. The point, it seems to me, is that to say what you want to say about something—in Trilling's case the idea of death, in my case the fictional detection of murder—you eliminate all those factors that bring in their wake complications detracting from your major aims. A Laskell or a Kate Fansler who was Jewish, married, worried about money, and embroiled in the twists and turns of an academic department would not do at all for either of us.

I find this fact amusing because I now know that Trilling and I had no common ground in ideas about politics, human destiny, women, or the role of the university; we shared only the necessity to transform our heroes into fantasy figures who would then be free to cope with profound perplexities, above all to be the sort of individual who would be committed to engaging with such matters. In picking the names for our protagonists, however, I chose one wholly unfamiliar to me. Laskell, on the other hand, bears a strong resemblance to Lionel, a name Trilling resented because it was too fancy. Turned into the name of a fictional character, it seemed quite appropriate.*

Unlike Trilling, I did not consider one's early thirties to be the middle of life's journey—though, sadly, thirty-five would turn out to have been the exact middle of Trilling's life; forty-two, Trilling's age when he wrote the novel, was in my view closer to the middle of the journey. I would later come to understand that women's life-changes occur noticeably later than men's.

The death of Laskell's not-quite-fiancée, Elizabeth, in her twenties, which occurred some time before the opening of the novel, was a sudden wholly unexpected death, as will be the death of the child, Susan. (Susan's death, of course, has been adumbrated by discussions of her heart trouble, though we hardly anticipate that her father will strike her dead.) The death of Elizabeth is a convenient device; leaving an attractive male character with a dead wife/lover is a clever way to allow him acceptable sexual activity while emphasizing his maturity in having committed his love to one woman in a genuine relationship. Laskell himself recognizes as a failure his not having committed himself to marrying Elizabeth, but that failure serves to underline the

---

*I discovered, however, many years after I had named my detective, that I had all unknowingly connected myself to the Hiss-Chambers case. Priscilla Hiss wrote to ask me how I had chosen the name "Fansler," since it was her maiden name. She mentioned that her sister had been a lecturer in art at the Metropolitan Museum. Then the name I had thought to have plucked out of the air revealed its source: my mother had sometimes taken me, as a child, to lectures at the Metropolitan, and the name Fansler must have rooted itself in my mind.

tentative quality of all his relationships. Had they been married and lived together, his absence at her death would not have been so blame-worthy; nor would she have called her sister rather than him when she so suddenly fell ill. As with Laskell's non-Jewishness, his freedom from marital ties leaves him able to speak and act with a freedom a married Jewish character could not have allowed himself.

My detective, Kate Fansler, was, unlike a male character, allowed simply to eschew marriage as a sign of courage rather than of an avoid-ance of commitment; she can be compared in this respect with P. D. James's series detective Adam Dalgleish, who, male-like, must be freed by having had his wife die in childbirth. Male and female char-acters require different stories to allow for similar outcomes along with their enactment of different kinds of courage. Certainly Trilling's and my experience of an ongoing marriage, complex and fraught with many difficulties as most marriages are, would have tilted our stories sharply away from the themes and, in my case, the frivolous entertain-ment we wished our books to embody.

Much about Laskell is compelling, particularly in light of Trilling himself. Why does Laskell, who admits to having originally wanted a literary career but exchanging it for architecture, know of himself that "he would never be great, [but] was reconciled to being useful"? This is an unlikely thought for a man such as Laskell or Trilling, but it is the sort of admission a woman might be forced privately to make — although "useful" for a woman would have a quite different mean-ing. Nonetheless, Laskell builds public housing, from concern for the poor, thus denying himself the possibility of greatness. Can Trilling have suspected that teaching, while certainly useful, rarely led to per-manent greatness such as that achieved by the dead authors he taught?

I must repeat that I do not mean to compare my first detective novel with Trilling's work in any substantial way. My intention is to notice how similar many aspects of the two novels are and to suggest, as I consider the influence of the fervently antifeminist Trilling in my life, that perhaps he so impressed his ideals and interpretations upon me because I recognized them as similar to my own — albeit, until now, unconsciously.

Both Trilling and I had comfortable enough childhoods but preferred more upscale backgrounds for our protagonists. Evidently, we both considered those from long-rich families to be living more at ease with their manners, their possessions, and their expectations of life; not seeking to impress anyone, they were, or seemed, freer to concentrate upon ideas and an unanxious enjoyment of amenities. Trilling, according to his wife, was as a child burdened with too much attention, too great expectations, and inappropriate clothes. He was not, like Laskell, simply the "well-loved child of the middle-class" but was smothered in the expectations of great achievement by his mother. I, the opposite of smothered, was given immense freedom and few material gifts, and, as a girl, was unburdened by any professional hopes for me. Both of us endowed our characters with a childhood we did not have — no worries about money or fear of spending it. Kate Fansler's parents are dead. We know nothing of where Laskell's parents are, although they must be assumed to be living; they don't enter into either his illness or his thoughts during his recovery. He is given a nurse, modeled upon an English nanny, as the female comforter throughout his illness. Above all, Laskell is allowed time minutely to examine his motives and actions with no major distractions. He is altogether unlike Trilling in not having demanding parents whom he had to support financially, a wife with recurring illness, complicated interactions in Columbia's English department (there were now no other kind, since the demise of those with the three-barreled names), worry about his writing, and what must have been his plans to have a child: James Trilling was born a year after the novel's publication.

And then there are, as I cannot resist mentioning, the double negatives, a form to which I have always been devoted; perhaps Trilling used them in his other writing and so I found pleasure in them there. Since copyeditors have been trying to wrest my double negatives from me all my writing life, I was delighted to discover Trilling's allegiance to them. Obviously, at least to him and me, they give a delicate shade of meaning that a simple positive statement could not achieve. For example, Crannock, the novel's setting, "was truly a town if only because it had a little common, rather scrawny, but not without charm, and even not without continuing use." Put plainly, without the double negatives, that description would accomplish but half the work. And Laskell, like Kate Fansler or any detective, is a protagonist who enters a situation, analyzes it, changes it, and then departs. In amusing myself by noting how much Laskell and Kate Fansler have in common, I am probably causing Trilling postmortem dismay; even if he could have understood that all the resemblances were superficial and did not imply comparable merit, literary or other, he would have despised so unseemly a comparison.

The two obvious literary influences on Trilling's novel are Henry James and E. M. Forster. The James influence is strikingly apparent in the extensive inner monologues, in the Jamesian habit of squeezing everything possible from a train of thought, and in giving the highest value to "awareness"—the major Jamesian quality stressed by Fadiman. It was, however, James's literary invention of what has been called the first/third method of narration that most influenced Trilling in the writing of his novel. Until the work of Henry James, novels were written either in the first person, as in David Copperfield—"I was born (as I have been told and believe) on a Friday at midnight"—or in the third person, otherwise called the omniscient narrator, as so famously in *Pride and Prejudice*—"It is a truth universally acknowledged that a single man in possession of a good fortune must be in want of a wife." James developed a third form: while the chief narrator is presented in the third person, his thoughts are rendered as though he were speaking in the first person, as in *The Ambassadors*—"This same secret principle, however, that had prompted Strether not absolutely to desire Waymarsh's presence at the dock, that had led him thus to postpone for a few hours his enjoyment of it, now operated to make him feel he could still wait without disappointment."

We are in the mind of Trilling's Laskell as we are in the mind of James's major characters. This central character observes what is going on, and everything that occurs in the story is told through his eyes. This technique of narration soon became widely employed, as is evidenced by the fact that most contemporary detective novels, if not presented in the first person, demonstrate its widespread use. Even where all action is not limited to the detective's observations, her or his thoughts follow the Jamesian first/third pattern.

Trilling's study of Forster, published in 1943, had taken note of Forster's use of sudden death, and of his delicacy in dealing with the subtle indications of actions and beliefs. Trilling did not know that Forster was homosexual when he wrote his study, and there can be little doubt that such knowledge might well have made the writing of the book impossible. As it was, Trilling was able, having perhaps noticed the skill in Forster, to observe and evaluate marriages, and to counter the general tendency to misjudge character too readily that Forster's novels so well demonstrated. Trilling eventually lost his admiration for Forster, and never mentioned him as an influential modernist. Forster was probably too "feminine," too sympathetic to women, too willing to allow his women to bear the central moral burden of his novels, for Trilling's wholehearted appreciation of him to endure. Forster, of course, turned out to have written about women in the absence of the opportunity to write about homosexuality. (Interestingly, the chronology of Trilling's life provided at the end of his festschrift omits the Forster book altogether, perhaps because the festschrift was edited by his students from a later time. It is also no surprise that the only woman-authored essay in the festschrift is by Gertrude Himmelfarb, that neoconservative reviler of feminism.)

Which brings me—no surprise—to the women in The Middle of the Journey. They are well drawn, but chosen throughout to provide a female reason for failure properly to respond or analyze. The exception is the girl child who, like the young girl in Trilling's story "The Other Margaret," is allowed to reach the wrong conclusions and learn the right ones. Why girls instead of boys? Obviously, the narrator's identification with a boy might be troublesome, as would the superior affection more safely offered to a girl; the whole relationship with a girl child could be more distant, less complicated. Similarly, dialogues unlikely to be imagined as comfortable or probable between men are made possible with the adult women:

> [Laskell] was embarrassed by having used the word life. He finished his sentence lamely—"to make certain demands on itself beyond its obvious needs."
>
> Nancy said, "I don't know what that means."
>
> "It makes requirements and sets limits to itself," said Laskell.
>
> "What does?"
>
> It was dreadful to have to say the word again, all by itself.
>
> "Life," he said. "It sets limits and it insists on acting with in them."
>
> He passionately wished he knew what he was talking about.

Emily, the woman Laskell will make love to only once and then refer to as his mistress, has "a womanly dignity that did not depend on intellect—a kind of biological intelligence." By the end of the novel, he will have come to despise her, for no expressed reason. Diana Trilling tells us, in *The Beginning of the Journey*, that "Lionel was unable to inject any note of tenderness" into the farewell encounter between Laskell and Emily. "Through rewriting after rewriting, Laskell was inexplicably angry at Emily." And, reminding us of Maugham's "The Treasure," which Trilling chose to include in his anthology of English literature, Laskell, having had sex with Emily, thinks "yet how much more grateful to Emily Caldwell he would now be if she would vanish, at this very moment, having made this strange, beneficent visitation of her."

Diana Trilling supplies a sad footnote to Laskell's interest in fishing and fishing equipment, an interest that Trilling shared. As she tells the story,

> I had a catastrophic social evening of my own connected with Lionel's trout fishing. Once, when he and Quentin Anderson and Jack Thompson and Charles Everett went off to fish together, I invited their wives to dinner. These were lively and gifted women but the venture was disastrous. Perhaps it was premature: this

was before women's liberation, and women had not yet imagined the possibility of a social engagement without men. We were not four women enjoying each other's company but four fishing widows putting ourselves in readiness for the funeral pyre.

It was not something he could imagine, or care to imagine. It is hardly to be wondered, then, that Trilling, unlike James or Forster, never shows us women together apart from men. Dorothy Sayers had pointed out, when complimented on her ability accurately to portray men speaking only to other men, that she assumed several intelligent men would not in fact speak to each other in a manner radically different from the way several intelligent women, when alone, would speak to each other. Trilling was, of course, in no way qualified to imagine the reverse of Sayers's insight. (It must, however, be granted that Sayers's intelligent English women were not, like those women at Diana Trilling's dismal dinner, academic wives lost without the men who gave them their identity.)

I find in the novel only two instances that remind me of the long-ago Trilling, the professor who taught me. The theme of death was one often mentioned in his lectures, and he was wont to sneer at America's attitude toward death; I remember his saying that we don't take children to funerals, as though death were somehow contagious—which is how the Crooms in his novel regard death. Then again, in the later introduction, Trilling refers to Chambers as a "man of honor," a description many people have long found puzzling, since Chambers was a spy. What Trilling apparently meant was that Chambers was not a man who would falsely accuse a friend; that is, his accusation of Hiss as a spy must have been true.

There is also a line in the book, reminiscent of all the old Trilling insightfulness, which is, oddly, spoken by the Chambers character, who says little else that is admirable. In a discussion of what is meant by God, Maxim says: "Suppose we say that God is the Being to whom things are rendered that are not rendered to Caesar." This seems to me accurately to represent Trilling's lifelong attempt to reconcile the value of bourgeois culture with his desire to overthrow so much of what it stood for. An agnostic, I find Maxim's one of the best definitions of spirit I have ever heard. And finally, I take perverse satisfaction in the fact that Trilling, disdaining Virginia Woolf as he did, in his novel nonetheless allows a moth to represent the incomprehensibility of death.

Trilling on Women

She never sought to distinguish herself in the world. . . .
She had no thought of making public use of her ready pen and her
powers of witty and robust observation. She did not even seek her social
life in the world of professional intellect. . . . She did not
become literary, she became an aunt.
LIONEL TRILLING, *"The Great-Aunt of Mr. Forster,"*
A Gathering of Fugitives

———

LIONEL TRILLING'S specific references to women, as writers, actors in society, or characters in novels, are few but telling. His thoughts on Jane Austen aside, his two essays, on Edith Wharton's *Ethan Frome* ("The Morality of Inertia," in *A Gathering of Fugitives*) and on Tess Slesinger's *The Unpossessed* ("Young in the Thirties") will allow me to encompass the subject of Trilling and women with more than adequate completeness. His *Ethan Frome* essay is, I think, a fine example of his style and of the adjudications that today seem so particularly pompous and unfeeling.

Compared to Fadiman and Barzun, Trilling was the instructor of my thought, my authority for how literary criticism should be written. Fadiman offered an example of how I might hope to write, Barzun provided kindly and invaluable instruction and support, but Trilling represented in his person and publications the very model of a literary personage grappling with a complex social world. That in reviewing his work now I find much of it unsatisfactory, indeed in some ways offensive, seems to speak volumes about what a young woman hoped for in the 1940s and '50s and what a mature feminist perceives today. His patronizing attitude toward Wharton, for example—"We can never speak of Edith Wharton without some degree of respect. She brought to her novels a strong if limited intelligence, notable powers of observation"—sounds as though he were discussing the paper of a promising graduate student.

Ethan Frome, which Trilling declares he had been induced into discussing, and has obviously agreed to discuss only for the chance to defame it, does not, he begins, deserve to be called "even a fine book": it is "factitious"; it is "a dead book, the produce of mere will, of the cold hard literary will. What is more, it seemed to me quite unavailable for any moral discourse. . . . It presents no moral issue at all." Never does he attempt to admit his blatant relish of the chance to devastate this woman author.

Nor can he let his disgust rest unbelabored; he must drive it home. "It suits Edith Wharton's rather dull intention to be content with telling a story about people who do not make moral decisions, whose fate cannot have moral reverberations." And again, "She was a woman in whom we cannot fail to see a limitation of heart, and this limitation makes itself manifest as a literary and moral deficiency of her work." "We" cannot help but notice "the deadness of her prose."

To answer the inevitable question as to why he did not refuse the invitation to discuss a book he considers so unworthy of attention, he explains that he will pronounce upon the problem of "inertia," not as Wharton has so annoyingly insisted on portraying it but as great men of the past have dealt with it. Trilling supposes the book is deemed of interest only because it has, for unworthy reasons he does not enumerate, come to be considered a classic. And indeed, Alfred Kazin, in his afterword to the edition I have of *Ethan Frome*, announces, some twenty-five years after Trilling's essay, that it "has long been an American classic," and that "no reader can escape [its] emotional force." (We might note here that Diana Trilling's essay honoring Wharton's intelligence and skill as a writer goes some way to indicate the eccentricity of Trilling's judgments on Wharton's work and reputation.)

Between Trilling's and Kazin's essays, of course, came feminism—not in this case a political movement but, rather, a literary revolution characterized by a recognition that the male approach to texts, and male assumptions, may be seen to have interfered with intelligent understanding of what is often a subtext or a different, formerly un-recognized point of view. Kazin takes no particularly "feminist" note of this in his 1987 afterword, but he does note that "what is important about Ethan, especially when compared with his wife, is his richer sensibility." He recognizes Wharton's ability "in the most gripping way, to project her dark view of marriage." He mentions her "increas-ing desperation at having to live with the inactive, difficult, envious Teddy Wharton," identifying her wish to live with a man of sensitivity and intuitive faculty similar to her own. Kazin believes that all Whar-ton's writing is driven by her necessity to write of doomed love. I con-sider this explanation reductive, but at least he understands that he is judging a book whose power invites explanation, not condescension.

I am reminded of Susan Glaspell's story "A Jury of Her Peers," little commented upon until the current women's movement brought it back into view, since when it has been frequently reprinted and studied. In this story, the wives of the men investigating a murder come to understand, as the male investigators do not, who committed the murder, and why. The men are content with their erroneous con-clusion that it was an intruder and not the man's wife who killed him, and the women do not dissuade their husbands from this conclusion. I mention the story here, not because it influenced Wharton's novel — it was published six years after Ethan Frome — but because it suggests the method of reading Wharton's novel demands and deserves.

Wharton ardently wished to become an acclaimed writer, and she probably believed that for a story to be accepted as a fine literary work it required a male protagonist. Yet how obvious it is that what she is portraying here is the sense of isolation, loneliness, and despair characteristic of rural women, isolated in farm houses, without near neighbors, companions, or affection. Such was the lot of the farmer's wife in Glaspell's story, which is why the woman's "peers" came to understand, from clues invisible to the men, why she murdered her husband. Ethan Frome is, so to speak, such a wife in drag — a crude way of saying that, seeking to portray female despair in a marriage, Wharton could allow herself to do so only if the despairing figure was a man. We have therefore the story of a desperate man, enticed by a sympathetic woman into the possibility of intimacy, but unable to find the means either to flee with her or to marry her. This is the story, of course, of *The Bridges of Madison County* and numerous other fictions of men suddenly appearing and offering impossible love to lonely women. To give herself even greater distance from her portrayal of a miserable woman in a miserable marriage, Wharton not only transformed her protagonist into a man but framed her story within the account of a male narrator — rather like the frame of *Wuthering Heights*.

Once one has grasped what is going on in this small novel, the hints thrown off by Wharton's unconscious seem almost obvious. So the narrator, when he first sees Ethan, wonders "how could any combination of obstacles have hindered the flight of a *man* like Ethan Frome" (my emphasis). The town has become so isolated that all who can have fled; why could not a "man" like Ethan flee? The answer, of course, lay in the fact that Wharton wished to portray the desolate imprisonment and isolation of a woman in such circumstances. She has created a man to stand in for a woman and has therefore given him no power. Since it was only women who were then without power, this ineffectualness helps to make Ethan oddly quirky as a male figure. Kazin remarks that "Wharton would have us believe that all Ethan and Mattie needed to get away was fifty dollars." Here he misses the pivotal truth: a woman might perish for the lack of fifty dollars, but it is unlikely that a man would suffer similarly.

Let us look closely at Ethan: "He could show [Mattie] things and tell her things, and taste the bliss of feeling that all he imparted left long reverberations and echoes he could wake at will." Such an emotion is characteristic of a lonely woman; indeed, many studies of adultery in women today reveal that, more than sex, it is the being listened to, talked with, encouraged to share their "reverberations and echoes" that women, ignored by inattentive husbands, desire. Again, to prevent Mattie's being sent off by his querulous wife, Ethan "even crept down on Saturday nights to scrub the kitchen floor after the women had gone to bed." Thinking of Mattie, he "abandons himself to dreams," like a woman reading a romance. Ethan had been trapped by having to care, first for his ailing father, then for his ill mother, then for his hypochondriac wife. This, a common enough female destiny, is certainly unusual for a man.

There is little point in expecting Trilling, or any other male English professor in the early 1950s, to have guessed the secret of the mysterious "factitiousness" Trilling found in Wharton's novel. But perhaps the reason Trilling felt such passionate repulsion from this work, and yet could not resist holding forth on its iniquities, was his profound distaste for any sensibility smacking of femaleness. Trilling published few literary diatribes, few harshly negative judgments of novels. That he chose to do so in the case of a woman author is significant, not least because he could convince himself he had been *requested* to write on Wharton: it had not been his choice, and he made clear his aversion to the assignment.

He was, of course, famously uninterested either in women students or in any women's writing apart from the universally excepted Jane Austen, and we have seen what views on women's moral life Austen inspired in him. His comments on the eponymous hero of Jane Austen's *Emma* are perhaps worth repeating here in full:

> Women in fiction only rarely have the peculiar reality of the moral life that self-love bestows. Most commonly they exist in a moonlike way, hinging by the reflected moral life of men. . . . They seldom exist as men exist—as genuine moral destinies. It is only on the rare occasions when a female character like Emma confronts us that the difference makes us aware of the usual practice. Nor can we say that novels are deficient in realism when they present women as they do: it is the presumption of our society that women's moral life is not as men's. *No change in the modern theory of the sexes, no advances in the status that women have made, can contradict this.* The self-love that we do countenance in women is of a limited and passive kind, and we are troubled if their self-love is as assertive as man's is permitted and expected to be. Not men alone, but women as well, insist on this limitation. (emphasis mine)

I do not suggest that Trilling had any great personal problem with women—I can't know whether he did or not; certainly his marriage was an unusually companionable one in the *Partisan Review* circle he inhabited—but he evidently could not imagine any literary work compelling his attention or admiration that was not demonstrably male in its characters and themes. Fadiman, as we have seen, felt the same way, but less passionately.

A slightly different project, however, casts another and more oblique light on Trilling's attitude toward literature and the women who write and appear in it. As the jacket copy on my edition of Trilling's *Prefaces to the Experience of Literature* (one of the three posthumous collections of Trilling's works edited by his wife) informs me, these introductory essays are from a textbook anthology for use in college courses in English and comparative literature, entitled *The Experience of Literature*. Apparently the multivolume anthology was unsuccessful for a beautifully ironic reason: Trilling's prefaces to each of the selections were so thorough and incisive that teachers were discouraged from using the text because they feared he had not left them anything to add. I can confirm this: in my first fulltime teaching job, at Brooklyn College, we used a text (this was long before the anthology) for which Trilling had written one of his perceptive introductions. A student simply lifted paragraphs from it for her term paper, apparently assuming that I would not myself have read or remembered the introduction, or would not be able to perceive the marked dissimilarity between the student's and Trilling's capabilities.

Looking over Trilling's prefaces forty-some years later, I am interested to discover that only one female fiction writer is included, Isak Dinesen. That Emily Dickinson is the only female in the poetry section is less startling—after all, even Fadiman admitted her talents—nor is it surprising to find no woman among the dramatists; I did, however, find it indicative that among Ibsen's plays Trilling chose *The Wild Duck*, a play with a largely masculine cast, and one whose theme—the dangers of insisting upon facing reality—Trilling compares with works of male writers through the ages. This from the most revolutionary of modern dramatists; would not most anthologists have chosen *A Doll's House*, or at least *Ghosts*? Well, this I might have passed over with little more than a sigh.

But for his lighter, more popular selection Trilling chose to include a story by Somerset Maugham, "The Treasure." This story, described by Trilling as "not serious," proposing "to do nothing but entertain," invites, as the Ibsen selection did, the question: why this particular story? And why Maugham? In answer to the second question, Trilling provides a stern critical dismissal of Maugham and then goes on to defend his choice. "The Treasure" recounts the unexpected sexual impulse of an upper class English bachelor, Harenger, who is suddenly overwhelmed by the desire to sleep with his perfect parlor maid. Next morning, appalled at the thought that she will take advantage of their intimacy and force him to let her go, he wonders what will he ever do without this gem of a servant? She is, it turns out, so perfect a gem that she makes no demands the following day; indeed, she acts as though nothing whatever has occurred. The bachelor is wonderfully relieved.

Now what is the theme of this story? Why include it in an anthology that begins with Sophocles and ends with Robert Lowell? For this reason: "it refers to our sense of the high value of sexual impulse and the absurdity of social convention." For the man in the story sets "more store by his narcissistic love of comfort and orderliness than by his erotic satisfaction." The story, Trilling concludes, offers us the picture of "a vanished mode of life . . . nor has [America] countenanced for men the life of . . . self-regard that is so important to Harenger." That the parlor maid might have had a point of view is considered beyond contemplation by both Maugham and Trilling.

In 1967 or earlier, this seemed acceptable enough. True, it did not occur to Trilling that the "pleasures of habitual comfort," which he admits are "not to be despised," were in fact expected by the majority of men at this time, not from the perfect servant but from their wives. America did not sustain a servant class—neither did England by the time Trilling wrote his preface—but it did sustain the ideal of the "wife and mother," who for no pay, and perhaps infrequently rewarded by the husband's "sexual impulse," performed as parlor maid, laundress, childminder, cook, and chauffeur. This wife was probably the same class as her husband, but was, for all that, no less in a servant role. Trilling might have glanced at The Feminine Mystique, published in 1963, but his wife assures us that he had no interest in women's liberation, which she, in her last book, would call "the most successful revolution of our century."

The sexual impulses of fastidious men interested him; women as objects of that impulse did not inspire his attention, although, as his review of the Kinsey report testifies, he considered women as sexual partners deserving of sexual fulfillment, not mere objects of male sexual impulses and selfish satisfactions. The moral impulses of men did comprise the most central complexity of Trilling's writings, but these were represented for him in the conflicts between man's nature and the demands of civilization, between middle class conventions and the profound male urgencies that must be made to live with those conventions. In these conflicts he was, of course, reinforced by Freud's disclosures, illuminating the tragic state of modern man caught in cultural imperatives. It was Trilling's intelligent and literary way of grappling with such struggles that so profoundly attracted me when I first encountered him.

Yet the passage about Austen's Emma that I have just quoted was written ten years before the anthology prefaces appeared. Nothing in the interim seems to have swayed Trilling to modify his views on women's moral destiny. Thus, he included "The Treasure" in his anthology, he says, because it was entertaining: representing evidence of woman's lack of "self-love" and man's right to his assertion of self-love apparently comprised for Trilling an "entertaining" concept. He finds it proper that the woman in Maugham's story does not demand any change in their relative status. Trilling denied that women too might be admired for self-love; he seemed to expect them to abjure any consideration of their own moral destinies.

I must emphasize that I do not mean that Trilling, in his personal life, wished to treat his wife or any other woman as a servant. In his essay on Tess Slesinger's novel, The Unpossessed, although he has harsh things to say about Slesinger's "feminist" ideas, he also expresses both sympathy and admiration for her. I suggest that this is because he knew her and therefore could not permit himself to think of her exclusively as a literary character or writer, however much he criticizes her on the basis of a literary idea. Apart from those he knew personally, he managed to remain ignorant of the condition of women who were not Diana Trilling or Tess Slesinger or Mary McCarthy. I have come to understand that he chose to have no insight into the conditions facing his women students, when he had any, or any compunction about how his ideas about women might disturb them.

I have mentioned that Trilling knew Tess Slesinger, and his attitude toward her novel and her views on women is necessary to complete my portrait of Trilling and women in the years when I was acquainted with him. Trilling had met Tess Slesinger at her marriage in 1928 to his friend Herbert Solow. During the first year of the Trillings' marriage, Slesinger and Solow decided to get divorced. (She would remarry happily and have a child.)

Diana Trilling relates the occasion of this divorce in *The Beginning of the Journey*. Herbert Solow "asked Lionel and me to be the witnesses of his trumped-up adultery." Adultery was at that time the only even moderately accessible or acceptable grounds for divorce. The "grounds" were faked, arranged so that witnesses who had been summoned could then testify to the adultery. As Diana Trilling continues, "we were to surprise him in his flagrant act. Lionel suggested that it would perhaps be more convenient for us if we came to Brooklyn on a Saturday afternoon instead of a weekday evening. 'The afternoon?' Herbert repeated in dismay. 'Am I to be perverse as an adulterer?'" Clearly, the Trillings knew Tess and her husband well.

I find it fascinating to compare Trilling's comments on Tess Slesinger's novel, written at the time I first encountered him at Columbia, with Janet Sharistanian's 1984 interpretation both of Slesinger's novel and of her life. I assume, at the time I write, that these later interpretations reflect attitudes toward women accepted by all but the most reactionary of individuals.

Here is Trilling in 1966 offering his views on feminist history as he discusses *The Unpossessed*:

> For some decades before the Thirties, the belief prevailed that woman stood in a special and privileged relation to "nature," or, as it was sometimes called, "life." Many writers [here he names most the famous modernists he had taught and/or admired] had contributed to a rather engaging mystique of Woman which developed concomitantly with the feeling that the order of the world as it had been contrived by man was a dismal and possibly a doomed enterprise. The masculine mind, dulled by preoccupation, was to be joined and quickened by the Woman-principle, which drew its bright energies from ancient sources and sustained the hope of new things. Implicit in the *mystique* was a handsome promise made to women—they were to be free, brilliant, and, in their own way, powerful, and, like men, they were to have destinies, yet at the same time they would be delightful, and they would be loved because they were women. The *mystique* faded and the promise lapsed. There are no traces of them in our contemporary literature. . . . But up through the Twenties, the *mystique* and its promise could still command the belief of some women.

Most important to note here is the tone: ironic, disdainful, relieved. All this has been proposed but soon seen for the nonsense it is and discarded. He is happy to tell us what followed. One must notice particularly the nouns and verbs he has chosen, as usual, with great care (I have italicized them).

> The American litigation between the sexes, after having been quite overt and articulate, has gone into a latent phase, but not before it produced a judgment against women that has *established* itself in our structure of belief. The substance of this judgment is that women are hostile to men and carry their hostility to the point of being *castrating*. . . . And here, it will occur to some readers to remark, is the archetypical female fantasy: the woman in

her specifically feminine role puts on power, becomes more powerful than the man; in the metaphor of her own *perverse mythology*,
she is the sun to the moon of the frightened and bewildered husband; nor does the *fantasy of power* stop short of her assumption
of a *masculine godhead.*

Reading these words at the present time, I am astonished to discover
how perfectly they reflect the male view, the Freudian view of women,
as it was generally established during my years as a graduate student
and as an assistant professor.

A major theme of the Slesinger novel is the inability of men either
to love or to connect their political ideals with their personal lives.
About this theme Trilling observes that "The failure of men to possess
the women is consonant with the inability to surrender themselves to
the ideals they profess." Today the verb "to possess" stops me in my
tracks, but it came readily to Trilling's pen as a description both of
the proper relationship between the sexes and of sexual intercourse.

Here then is how Trilling ultimately dispatches Slesinger's novel:

> *The Unpossessed*, quite apart from its *parti pris* [its feminist lean-
> ings], is avowedly and unabashedly a woman's novel and that lack
> of substantiality of which I have complained is in part the re-
> sult of a woman writer's stylistic intention—gross and weighty
> facts were to be kept to a minimum so that there would be little
> impediment to the bright controlled subjectivity of a feminine
> prose manner inaugurated by Katherine Mansfield and given au-
> thority by Virginia Woolf, and used here with a happy acerbity of
> wit superadded.

The tone of irony and mild contempt is particularly evident in the
final phrases of this sentence. Needless to say, Trilling had no use for
Virginia Woolf, who may have "given authority," but, he implies, to
whom, and for what sad purpose?

We turn now to Professor Janet Sharistanian's afterword to the 1984
reissue of Slesinger's novel. Sharistanian doesn't refer to Trilling's
piece, even while she contradicts it at many points; since her bibli-

ography is notably complete, and since she refers to Trilling in other connections, it is probable she didn't know of this particular article whose title does not mention Slesinger. (Sharistanian does, however, note that Fadiman had advised Slesinger on her manuscript, and subsequently became her editor at Simon and Schuster.)

Here is how Sharistanian interprets the contemporary reviews of *The Unpossessed*, an assessment that applies equally well to Trilling's article. Sharistanian suggests that Slesinger's political ambivalence in the novel had displeased reviewers because it "included a feminist perspective [that] exacerbated the reactions against her." It is of course also true that, while Trilling perceived Slesinger's ambivalence to be between men and women, earlier reviewers had interpreted that ambivalence as hostile to socialism, suggesting that Slesinger approved it insufficiently.

"The novel is not a polemic," Sharistanian insists, because Slesinger pays close attention to both the man's and the woman's "lonely thoughts, churning emotions, and genuine suffering." "Yet," she adds, echoing Trilling's objections but rescuing them from condemnation, "there are also some special similarities among the female characters: they are lost souls in a male ideological universe that refuses to see women."

There can be no doubt of Slesinger's feminism. When she and Solow were divorced, she moved to Hollywood with her second husband to become a screen writer. There she wrote the screenplays for, among other films, *The Good Earth* and *A Tree Grows in Brooklyn*. She also wrote what Sharistanian calls "a proto-feminist film," entitled *Dance, Girls, Dance*; it was directed by Dorothy Arzner, Hollywood's only female studio director. Slesinger's interest in feminism is further implicit in an unproduced script she and her husband wrote, based on the life of Elizabeth Blackwell, the first woman doctor in the United States.

"Unfortunately," as Sharistanian quotes Mary Anne Ferguson's words, Slesinger had "everything but time"; she was dead before her fortieth birthday. And yet, Sharistanian goes on to claim, "her one published novel offers its own form of literary timelessness. Lively, even controversial in Slesinger's own day, *The Unpossessed* has survived to become a feminist classic in ours." As Sharistanian sums it up, "The story points toward the difficulties of self-expression by the more sympathetic characters of both sexes in *The Unpossessed* and the special difficulties the female characters have in making any claims for themselves upon the world."

However idle it is to do so, one can but wonder what else Slesinger might have written. The last chapter of *The Unpossessed*, which had first been published as a short story, and became a celebrated one, relates the abortion the central female character is forced to have because her husband wants neither to have nor to deal with a child. This was perhaps the earliest abortion in an American novel; it caused the original story to be often rejected. Trilling does testify to the fact that "the intellectuals of the Twenties and Thirties were likely to assume that there was an irreconcilable contradiction between babies and the good life." But he does not seem to find this ambiguity deserving of the power with which Slesinger endows it.

Trilling's "Young in the Thirties" is valuable for the light it casts on political life in that decade, and particularly on the life of intellectual, nonreligious Jews of that period, as I have suggested. Insofar as the article expresses Trilling's views on women, their condition, their recent history, and their hopes for change, it encapsulates with eerie perfection his lack of imagination when it came to women, and his failure, or profound disinclination, to sympathize with them and their lot. As Morris Dickstein said of Trilling, he "wrote as a man speaking to men."* And in his book on Trilling Mark Krupnick mentions that "Trilling took seriously the notion that he was educating young men — he was never much concerned with the education of young women — who would, as he dismissively put it, be 'responsible for the welfare of the polity.'"

Perhaps it was because of her fervent interest in the education of young women that Trilling, according to Krupnick, disliked Virginia

---

* Morris Dickstein in his 1977 *Gates of Eden* managed, quite in the Trilling style, to refer to few women and to mention the women's movement only once, dismissing it as an "inward" movement.

Woolf. However responsible for the polity Woolf or any other woman might be, Trilling did not consider them to be central to the difficulties inherent in the modern condition. In "Some Notes for an Autobiographical Lecture," an appendix to *The Last Decade*, he asks: "How could one read Yeats or Joyce or Lawrence or Eliot or Proust or Mann or Kafka without understanding that the culture of humanism was at a point of crisis?" That the conduct concerning women was at the center of that point of crisis and, indeed, that fear of the rising of women's voices was the motivation for much of the crisis as these modern writers saw it, did not so much as occur to Trilling.

What is particularly troubling is not just his dislike of feminists, nor his horror of women intruding upon male power, nor his failure even to notice the struggle of women to be recognized by such as himself, but his intensity on this subject, and the fact that never in his lifetime did he alter or modify these opinions.

As I write this, I wonder how I coped with this attitude of Trilling's during all those early years when I so admired and eagerly followed his example of what I wanted to be and how I wanted to think. I knew he detested any extended interpretation or defense of women characters in the books he lectured upon. He once told me, in answer to a question about women after one of his lectures, that I ought to forget this subject and not harp on it. Until the women's movement gained momentum, I followed his advice, or hoped to follow it, though there is some evidence in my publications that I was not altogether compliant. Perhaps my silence was why he allowed me to gain tenure in 1966—the year he published "Young in the Thirties."

He suspected me of feminism, but he did not, I now suppose, consider it possible that such views could last or could ever become influential or have any notable impact upon Columbia's English department. I did, I believe, have an effect, though less far reaching than I would have liked, upon that department, but that was after Trilling's death and, as he, remembering Marlowe, might have thought of it, "in another country."

DIANA TRILLING

Lionel felt of my work that it was not enough
appreciated and that this was chiefly due to his presence in
my life. . . . He would point out to me . . . that there was no
other woman writer in our circle who was so
unremittingly coupled with a man as I.
DIANA TRILLING, The Beginning of the Journey

————

WHEN I BEGAN this rumination on three men who had, in the absence of any available female patterns for the life I desired, become my examples of how such a life was led, I had no thought of writing extensively about Diana Trilling. To my surprise, in reading her writings for clues about Fadiman, Trilling, and Barzun, I found myself with a new appreciation of her struggles and achievements: these have been little noticed. Those who wrote of Diana Trilling, and those who over the years I heard talking of her, found no reason to appreciate or praise her. Almost every reference to her that I have read is negative, portraying her as lacking any intellectual power, unimportant, querulous, difficult, flawed.

Perhaps she was an awkward or annoying person. Certainly at Columbia all I heard of her left the impression that she was carping, demanding, exacting, unworthy of Lionel.* After his death, at the lectures offered in Lionel's name, the impatience she evoked in men such as Steven Marcus became palpable: I remember the way he spoke to her from the podium, in response to some objection she had made. The sympathies of the audience at that time were clearly all with him, though I can remember none of the details. She interested me so little

———
*In this chapter, I shall refer to the Trillings as Diana and Lionel, not out of inappropriate familiarity but to speak of them separately with ease.

that I had no desire to learn about her, either when I was at Columbia or when I began writing this book.

Why should I think about her now? She was certainly no influence, no model; if anything, she seemed to offer the opposite of any existence I might have hoped for for myself. This conviction was reinforced when she published *Claremont Essays* in 1964. Although Lionel was no longer at the center of my thoughts, nothing relating to him failed to interest me. I picked up Diana's book of essays and put it down in disgust, chiefly I think because of a wrongminded and unperceptive essay on Virginia Woolf, whose writings were already captivating me, albeit in secret; I believed hers to be the great not-yet-discovered voice of modernism. Rereading that essay today, I still find it unacceptable, but I am able to put it in historical perspective. In 1948, when Diana's essay on Woolf was first published, Woolf represented in most English departments, and certainly to Lionel, an attenuated, over-delicate sensibility, one that had an unfortunate influence on otherwise worthy women writers such as Tess Slesinger. Even in 1964 Woolf was hardly the prominent figure she was to become in later years, but I found Diana's words on her inexcusable. I put Diana's book away; she literally never entered my mind for almost three decades.

My next encounter with Diana came when she published *The Beginning of the Journey* in 1993. Asked by the *Boston Globe* to review it, I read it with passionate interest: the subtitle was "The Marriage of Diana and Lionel Trilling"; how could I not hasten to learn more about Lionel and about Columbia? I found myself sympathetic to Diana in that book, and for the first time began to think about, indeed even to understand, what it must have meant for a woman of talent and high intelligence to be Lionel's wife. I have not studied the matter in detail, but I have the impression that *The Beginning of the Journey* was received with more resentment than appreciation. Even John Rodden, who had interviewed Diana, apparently with appreciation, for his book on Lionel's critics, nonetheless described *The Beginning of the Journey* as "a vinegary memoir" written with "a kind of rough love." He insists that Diana "berates" Lionel, and refers to her as "girding for battle against both old and new political foes." She was obviously held in low esteem before anyone read her book, and was considered guilty of hubris in discussing herself in the same breath, so to speak, with Lionel.

As I pursued my memories of Fadiman, Trilling, and Barzun, I read everything Diana had published, not yet in search of her in her own right but to round out my studies of the three men. I found myself surprised by the positive impressions of her I was gaining. Stunned by the responses of those to whom I mentioned my new and still grudging admiration for her, I became troubled by how wildly disliked or disdained she seemed to have been, and how little appreciation of her was to be found in published materials about the Trillings' circle. I have no doubt that having been married to Trilling was both the greatest opportunity for, and the dominant restriction upon, Diana's life as a female writer and thinker. Little of this was, I believe, Lionel's fault. The times, as she so well understands in all she writes, were not conducive to a woman's professional development. How certainly I knew this; was it not with this knowledge that I had adopted my three male models, models I was never able to call mentors?

Diana was twenty years older than I, yet her experiences as a girl and as a college student—I mean, of course, not her personal conditions but the culture of the times—were hardly different from mine. Radcliffe in 1923 and Wellesley in 1943 were amazingly similar in their assumptions about women's lives and in their lack of any expectation of female autonomy. So I might say that, in hindsight, I came to "identify" with her, as I never identified with any of the three men: I found that I easily recognized her situation and understood how she had suffered from intellectual frustration. In her case, that suffering manifested itself in illness and psychosis.

I am hardly in complete accord with her about feminism; if we started in the same place, twenty years apart, we ended in quite different places. Nonetheless, unlike any of the famous women she knew, she does allow the truth about women's lives to enter into her writings; she admits to being a woman like other women. More important to me, she does not consider herself to be "one of the boys," and therefore perfectly entitled to scorn other women who to do not "belong" in the world of the *Partisan Review*.

When I read Diana's essays and books, it is no effort to find areas of disagreement. As with Lionel, her views on communism and Joseph McCarthy are exactly opposite to those of my generation of liberals. But unlike anyone else in her circle, from Lionel to Hannah Arendt, she is capable of transforming her ideas, of reconsidering long held views, and of expressing sympathy for those unlike herself. Diana willingly undertook patient reading through reams of testimony: in her essay on Robert Oppenheimer and her book *Mrs. Harris*, she both modified her impressions because of this careful reading and reported on those modifications. Furthermore, she was, however opinionated, not, like McCarthy and Arendt, dedicated to witty unkindness for its own sake. And where she disagreed with Lionel, or could be found to contradict him, I usually found her view the more persuasive.

Above all, for me, Diana's is one of the few female voices today recalling, with an insight born of rejection and of her marriage to one of the male masters, her generation's experience of male rule. When I saw the play *Copenhagen* by Michael Frayn, I saw reflected in the figure of Niels Bohr's wife the role Diana played in the life of Lionel and his male circle. The play imagines a meeting between Bohr and Heisenberg years after the war; they recall their encounter during the war when they had met for reasons no one knows, but presumably to discuss the making of the atomic bomb. The men argue, and Bohr's wife, whom Bohr obviously loves and holds in great respect, is able to recall details of the earlier encounter and set it in context. So, I suggest, Lionel and his colleagues, at Columbia and in their circle outside Columbia, were also observed by a woman who understood a great deal, who was valued by her husband, but who was never considered one of the major players. Such a person holds an essential key to the historical past.

Here, it seems to me, is a matter of considerable interest and significance. Though Diana was an observer of the major intellectual figures of the time, including her husband who was a central player, it has occurred to no one to take her perceptions and conclusions with any seriousness. Rather, they are dismissed as mean, silly, and insignificant. Yet, just as Bohr's wife in *Copenhagen* turns out to have understood all that had gone on, and remembered and analyzed more than had either of the men, so Diana watched and remembered and reported. This should be of value to historians of that time, rather than a matter for scorn. For me, Diana's views cast an illumination that, in the end, I came to consider indispensable as I reconsidered these men and the place they occupied in my life and aspirations so long ago.

Diana began publishing late in life. Like so many women of her generation or mine, she felt no impulse toward a professional life, or no continuing impulse. She had an operatic voice and many talents, but being a wife was, as it was for most women then, the central feature of her being. The difference between her generation and mine, however, was the culturally supported impetus to have children. That Diana and Lionel were forty-three when their only child was born would have been an almost impossible situation in my day. My generation of women were expected to start having babies early and to devote themselves entirely to domestic matters and volunteer services. The alumnae notes for my Wellesley class over the years confirm this fact. Intentionally waiting until I was nearly thirty to have my first child, I was harried unmercifully in the years preceding my, at that time, tardy pregnancy. Aside from the pressure to have children, however, Diana and I faced the same college experience, the same world, and the same expectations or lack thereof.

Diana was thirty-six when Lionel recommended her as book reviewer for the *Nation*, a position that seems to have long been occupied by a series of Columbia College graduates and their wives. A true wife of her time, Diana admitted that if Lionel "had indicated any doubt of my ability to do the work, I would have at once withdrawn my candidacy." Once she set off on a career as a writer of reviews and critical articles, however, she learned, as few women then had the opportunity to learn, that work is the only force beside love that is essential to the lived life (Freud had, of course, perceived this, though not about women). As Diana put it, "even with Lionel at my side, it was my writing which gave the middle years of my life much of their focus and meaning and since his death it is my work which has sustained me at an age when lack of purpose is the death of the living."

Widows who have never worked outside the home rarely experience a miserable old age, despite widespread assumptions to the contrary: such widows, indeed, as reported in longitudinal studies, are often the happiest of women. For the first time they can allow themselves to feel in control of their lives and their time. But men or women in retirement from a professional life suffer in a specific way, discovering with Diana that "lack of purpose is the death of the living." Having taken for granted that their work signified their purpose in life, they now are left adrift, worried about their place in the world and uncertain what any new work might be, or how their new life might encompass it.

Of the women in the *Partisan Review* circle, however, only Diana had not seen work as the major dedication of her life. Of these women, only Hannah Arendt was left a widow, and certainly her work continued to sustain her. The others in the group, such as Mary McCarthy and Elizabeth Hardwick, had so many lovers and husbands that the category of "widow" hardly applied. In addition, they had all been professionals throughout their lives, which is perhaps why they never ceased to scorn Diana as a "mere wife," even when, as a widow, she became a fulltime professional writer. Well before her widowhood, she accepted her wifely role as inevitable in that period. Lionel, however, did understand the necessity she felt for something beyond domesticity, and this must have comforted her.

Through Diana's account of her marriage and of Lionel throughout those years, an ardent if past admirer of Lionel's is for the first time offered a portrait of him that is not the one he presented to his students or to the world. As we have seen, Diana was well aware of Lionel's character as perceived by his students and by me; she understood his place in the fantasies of his students and in the ideals of readers beyond Columbia. She observes, however, that Lionel concealed his shortcomings from his students, fearing they would respect him less if, for example, they knew that he experienced psychic obstacles and was in analysis. She understood the importance to Lionel of his image as a person in control of his life, and she wonders, if Lionel had lived to write his memoirs, whether or not he would have examined the problems his "image" caused him.

As I grew older and entered Lionel's profession, or what he would have considered my eccentric version of his profession, I identified with him less and less. Yet he never ceased to be my model in his respect for his profession and the seriousness with which he took literature. I might once have aspired to imitate his aloofness, but the changes feminism brought persuaded me rather to offer its mirror image: I wanted no student of mine to be rejected as I felt Lionel had, in my earliest graduate years, rejected me. I wish I could have known a few more details about him that would have made him appear human as I was human. To take just one instance, I learned in 1993 from Diana's book that Lionel discovered, at a ball, that "dancing to rock 'n' roll released him from the necessity of leading a partner and this enchanted him." By 1966, when Lionel made this discovery, I too had decided that having to follow a man did not allow me to express my delight in dancing; I too found enormous the attraction of dancing with someone, moving together with him, but apart.

Diana's version of her marriage to Lionel—and there is never the story of a marriage, only versions of it—seems to me remarkably to capture the tensions that then faced an ambitious woman, particularly one who wished to remain in her marriage and could not at first contemplate a professional life that any husband in those days might be presumed to discourage. The devotion of those two—despite many struggles and much anguish—renders their marriage unique in the circles in which they moved, including both Lionel's colleagues and the *Partisan Review* crowd. With all the nastiness directed at Diana, no one suggests that either she or Lionel followed the life of sexual promiscuity or infidelity for which the others were famous. In saying this, I do not wish to be seen as disapproving of the behavior of McCarthy, Hardwick, Rahv, and the rest; moral strictures are not here the point, nor do I condone such strictures. At the same time, the fact of this devoted marriage certainly says something about Lionel and Diana that we must honor. Diana was for some years racked by disease, much of it undoubtedly psychosomatic and caused by the stresses of being a woman in that sorry time. Lionel, she tells us, in those years did unmanly housework and took care of his disabled wife. Diana's account of their marriage rings true:

> We were never in love in the way that people are in love in popular songs. . . . Over a long lifetime, we loved each other very much, increasingly over the years, although in middle life we quarreled a great deal and often threatened each other with divorce. But even at our angriest we were never estranged, we never stopped talking with entire intimacy, and there was never a time or situation in which we could not trust and count on each other.

She recognizes that with her upbringing she had to marry a man who was more successful than she; she believes that she could not have managed a marriage in which this was not the case. And, as she exactly puts it for herself—and me: "That the addition of a professional job to a woman's homemaking occupations demands the expenditure of double energies was not a subject which was much discussed in my generation. . . . There was nothing special about this. It was the way that nice girls were raised." Yet we must notice that when Diana was too ill for housework, Lionel did it: reluctantly, clumsily, but he did it. Similarly, because of her illness he was not drafted for World War II in 1941, a great loss to him, who yearned to experience just such a rite of manhood; he always regretted that missed opportunity.

Nor does she blame Lionel for her "failure to engage in a larger enterprise than reviews and articles." The failure, she insists, was hers, not, as was widely supposed, attributable to Lionel's presence in her life. After his death she did, of course, publish two full-length books, *Mrs. Harris* and her account of their marriage. My belief, which I mentioned in my review of *The Beginning of the Journey*, is that she would have made her life easier had she decided, when she began as a reviewer, to write under her birth name. Their friends at *Partisan Review*, she tells us, were "united in the advice that I write under my maiden name; they feared that I was going to be an embarrassment to Lionel.

But Lionel was adamant that I write as his wife." It seems obvious that if she had not feared being an embarrassment to Lionel, and if his insistence had not been designed to counter that fear, the name "Diana Rubin" would have served everyone better; certainly it would have taken her more directly out of his shadow. Can that have been what both of them feared?

From Diana's memoir, we learn that Lionel eventually tired of teaching and of the position he was required to maintain. We learn also of the difficulty he experienced in writing. Many were shocked when his son, James, published an article insisting that Lionel, like James himself and like Lionel's father, had suffered from what is now called attention deficit disorder. Whether or not this is the correct diagnosis in Lionel's case, he certainly agonized over his writing to a degree suggesting some deep conflict or affliction. I learned also, though I hardly needed Diana to tell me this, that late in his life Lionel responded with sadness to the distance he now perceived between himself and his students, and to the temper of the times, so greatly changed from the temper of the times in which he had flourished.

"It never ceases to surprise me how little able intellectuals are to apply their gifts of mind to life's actualities or, even more important, how little their strength of mind is matched by grace and generosity of spirit." So Diana wrote. She was speaking of intellectuals in a general way, noticing their frequent failure to be people of reason or imagination. Her description, however, seemed to me amazingly relevant to the personalities, speech, and actions of the former students of Lionel's who became my colleagues at Columbia. They seemed no more ready than Lionel to consider ideas they had not arrived at before they were thirty-five; because of the times in which they flourished, unlike the years of Lionel's sway, this disability doomed the English department to years of strife, disorganization, and ill-feeling.

The cause, of course, was the growing power and influence of women. Lionel could ignore this, but they, who could not, erected a stone wall to keep it at bay. This was hardly effective, but it did manage to discourage the women and debilitate the men. I was, therefore, intrigued to discover that Diana embraced, though never in a confrontational way, many ideas Lionel would hardly have endorsed, often on the subject of women and feminism. Although she must have noticed his refusal ever (except for his essay on *Emma*) to discuss the changing—in his view, unchanging—role of women, she never mentions it. The ideas that led me to reconsider her as a person were never offered as criticisms of Lionel: if her accounts of her domestic arrangements owed their insights to feminism, she never blamed him. Rather, she blamed the stereotypical wifely role almost unavoidable for a woman of her generation.

Diana writes, "Women's liberation, that most successful revolution of our century, has cast a wide net. By now it reaches even the aging men of my generation." She is not here thinking of Lionel, who did not live to become an aging man in his seventies or beyond. She also notes—and one can but wonder what Lionel would have made of this —"There is small doubt that Freudian doctrine, often scarcely understood, has greatly powered the development in recent decades of what amounts to virtually an antifemale movement in American culture." How right she is! The ardent Freudians, those I taught among and those I read, may recognize Freud's misogyny, but only to pay it lip service. Privately, profoundly, they think that Freud was right about women. I sense that Lionel thought so too.

Diana's statements about Freud carry particular weight when one considers the years she spent in analysis with a variety of analysts who sound one more destructive than the other. That is, I admit, an impression I am ready to receive, since my own memories of the women I knew who were committed to analysis confirm Diana's experiences. Because these memories are no longer exact, I report, as a substitute, Maxine Kumin's anger at Anne Sexton's encounters with analysts. Kumin is surprised at the way Martin Orne, who rescued Sexton from a mental institution and encouraged her to begin writing, is pilloried by his colleagues for giving tapes of his sessions with Sexton to Sexton's biographer. Kumin writes:

I have never been able in my own mind to sort out the truths from the half-truths in this issue; the love affair her second psychiatrist conducted with her over a two-year period—sessions for which he was paid—earned this shrink not even a reprimand. And psychiatrist number three, who permitted Sexton to go off her medication and soon thereafter resigned from the case without finding her a suitable substitute, seems the most reprehensible of all.

Diana's experiences with analysts are hardly better; none understood her anguish or helped her, as she reports, in any way. Since feminism, one happily notes, psychoanalysts have markedly changed their attitudes toward and assumptions about women patients.

She came eventually to realize that "the ready ridicule of women's liberation is confirmation that women are indeed regarded in our society as of a second order of being and that we are reluctant to have this truth revealed to us. By 'us' I of course mean women as well as men." The last sentence here is characteristic of Diana: she fears, as so many women do, that to blame the patriarchal system for women's secondary position in life is somehow to blame men, a sex it is dangerous to offend and not all of whose members are, in fact, against women's liberation. Yet she is no longer persuaded that women are biologically determined to passivity; rather, she now tends to see women's passivity as the result of cultural conformity or laziness. This is surely a revolutionary statement from one of her generation of women who, if successful, scorned other women and jeered at feminism. I was moved by her observation of what Solzhenitsyn's *Cancer Ward* makes clear: that a woman surgeon in the Soviet Union, though she returns home to do all the domestic work, does not find "in her home and family but in her 'real' work—her man's work, if you will—her chief pride."

Unwilling to condemn men in any general ways, she finds herself more troubled by "the petty superiorities which men assert over women than by the grand social injustices. . . . With my reliable sense of direction, I have to yield to a male navigator determined to drive us a hundred miles out of our way." She looks forward to the day when in our living rooms women "are naturally paid the same heed, given the same credence, as men can now count on for their opinions and speculations." This hope resonates profoundly with a female professor such as myself who has, upon innumerable occasions at faculty meetings, offered suggestions that were ignored only to be later greeted with enthusiasm when repeated by a male member of the faculty. What Diana learned in her living room, I learned in academia. As Lionel's wife, as the hardly honored appendage to the great man, she must have suffered many instances of disrespect and exclusion. As David Laskin writes in *Partisans*, "she railed at how members of her generation, women as well as men, insisted on pegging her as 'Trilling's wife' and dismissed her as a 'marital appendage.'" Note the verb "railed." This is the kind of word usually used in describing Diana; even if there is implicit confidence in her utterances, they have to be undercut. And of course, all feminists rail, do they not?

I have here gathered together Diana's unexpected opinions on the subject of women; they are, in fact, scattered throughout her writings, which is perhaps why they have been so little noticed—if the reason is not simply that no one much notices her except in relation to Lionel. Laskin speaks of how Mary McCarthy soon became "one of the boys—accepted and respected as [Diana] never would be." When they first met, Laskin reports, McCarthy was struck with Diana's beauty, but "once she married Lionel, Diana ceased to register with Mary as either a beauty or a Trotskyite and devolved into a mere wife." Elizabeth Hardwick and Hannah Arendt also treated Diana brutally, dismissing her writings and inflicting on her what she called their "arrogance and condescension." Despite his subtle undercutting of Diana throughout his book, Laskin does end on a complimentary note about *The Beginning of the Journey*: she spoke, he writes, "with candor and clarity. She closed the book with a moving, unflinching elegy of the 'strange difficult ungenerous unreliable unkind and not always honest people who created the world in which Lionel and I shared.'" After Lionel's death, Diana looked at that those people in a new light and, outliving them, took the opportunity for revenge not earlier offered to her.

I end here with a passage from Diana's book *Mrs. Harris*. Diana does not retain, as the trial develops, the sympathy for Jean Harris as the scorned woman with which she had begun to follow the trial. Indeed, her book is both a moral judgment upon Jean Harris and, toward the end, an attempt to understand her as a woman who acted so astonishingly considering her position in life—as the headmistress of the fashionable Madeira School—and her role as a model of sophisticated WASP society. Diana writes:

> It's hard for me to imagine Jean Struven as a child or early adolescent. . . . Was she made jealous of privileges given a brother but withheld from a girl? When a girl is as mentally gifted as she was, the contradiction between ability recognized and ability hindered for no other reason than that of sex can be deeply painful; the idea of sexual injustice gets burnt into one's view of the world.

Diana goes on to envision Jean Struven at college in the early 1940s, "a particularly bad time in the history of American women." Women, Diana observes, and I can certainly verify this, weren't allowed to challenge the way power was distributed between the sexes. She goes on to rebut Freud's condescension to women and his irrefutability at that time; women were required to see the inevitable passivity that was attributed to them as the mark of their biology, the stigma of their sex.

The misjudgment of, the lack of appreciation for, Diana Trilling's insights and carefully wrought principles saddens me. I have the sense of few taking the trouble to read her work, particularly The Beginning of the Journey, beyond searching for her statements about Lionel, which they tend to consider as unworthy gossip and which they scorn. Yet her devotion to Lionel and to their marriage is palpable throughout the book. Lionel hid from almost everyone, perhaps literally from everyone except his analyst and Diana, his fears, his ineptitudes, his mounting regrets and sense of failure. He is fortunate that these shortcomings are presented by his wife as though they were somehow in the service of his preeminence, as one writes of a great man or woman whose human failings enrich rather than detract from their accomplishments.

Much of what I read about Lionel today dismisses him as, for example, does David Brooks in *Bobos in Paradise*. Brooks condemns Trilling and his generation of critics and thinkers as holding forth on topics "that would be regarded as pompous by most writers today." He finds that men such as Trilling and Barzun had "an exalted view of the social role of the intellectual" as "they issued the sort of grand and often vaporous judgments that today strike us as ridiculous."

For Diana, and for me, Lionel's "pompous topics" were the stuff of life. That Lionel's generation of thinkers did not look enough into the outside world of political movements is certainly true, though *pace* Brooks, Lionel was sharply aware of the world of commerce. I believe that if Lionel had been able to accept into his world view the phenomenal revolutions of his time—feminism and civil rights—he would have achieved a degree of greatness that was denied him. Unfortunately, many of his faithful male students, all like me now long in the tooth, still embrace Lionel's limitations and so cannot abide the world as changed by the last century's revolutions being forced upon them, as they see it, from outside Lionel's own distinctive moral universe.

He did not fail me in this way—precisely because I was a woman. I could not model myself upon him, I could not become like him. And so I moved with the times and did not continue to worship an idol whom time would defeat. But for me, and I think for Diana also, what he did offer, to her in marriage, to me in his tutelage, was an example of how as an intellectual one might grapple with the forces of an increasingly consumer-oriented, morally indifferent society. His was a powerful voice, and it is likely that, ironic as it seems, it is partly through women's literary work that that voice will continue to be heard. For if he did not recognize the complexity of women's lives, his way of presenting the "betweenness" of a life in conflict applies now to women as, then, it applied only to a man such as he was.

Jacques Barzun I

The detective tale is not the place to make us appreciate
the moral burdens of the times by presenting a detective
who is middle-aged, humane, and embittered.

JACQUES BARZUN, The Energies of Art

———

ON APRIL 4, 2000, Jacques Barzun, the only one of my three men still living, appeared at the New-York Historical Society to speak about his new book, *From Dawn to Decadence*. I wondered why there were no books to buy, and learned that apparently Barzun had insisted upon last-minute corrections, which had delayed the book's publication. The publisher, who had paid for the occasion, could hardly have been pleased: many of the large crowd who came to hear Barzun would probably have bought a copy at the now canceled reception. I was not surprised at the delay: Barzun had always been particular about his books, and this, the last, profited from his assiduous attention. At the end of the program, Barzun, holding a cane but not leaning on it, was greeted by many of the audience. I did not wait to talk to him, but wrote him a note about how much I had enjoyed his presence and his interview with Arthur Schlesinger, Jr., a mere youth of eighty something, who acted as interlocutor. Barzun, as he always had, answered my letter with one of his own. His courtesy toward me has always been amazing, undeserved, and welcome. To those who equate formality with arrogance, he often seemed off-putting in manner. To me, however, he has been the kindest of men.

When I came to read *From Dawn to Decadence* I was impressed with the book's clarity, intelligent internal references, and many other innovations that rendered the long work readable, useful, and cleverly arranged with cross references. So many books from which we recall some crucial point provide no means to rediscover it, either from its index or by any other means. From the point of organization, usefulness, and pleasure in reading, Barzun, whose advice to authors in books such as *The Modern Researcher* had been, I believe, the best available in all its details, had at last been allowed by a publisher to produce, at the end of his life, the perfectly written and organized book.*

Barzun's appearance in New York was the culmination of a schedule persons twenty or thirty years younger might have found arduous. He had devoted three days to a conference on Berlioz at Smith College, an occasion including a lecture, an appearance as guest of honor at a dinner, and participation in many meetings. In addition to the event at the New-York Historical Society, he spent four busy days in New York and Washington, where he was interviewed by Edward Rothstein of the *New York Times*, as well as at the Smithsonian Institution.

The *Times* interview, together with a large picture of Barzun smiling, refers to him as the "founder of cultural history as a distinct discipline." Speaking from his daughter's Manhattan apartment, Barzun recalled his impression of the United States while he was still in France: "I had read a lot of books about the Indians," he explained to the *Times* reporter; "I thought that I would come here and see Indians galloping across the plains." Barzun also referred to the only personal event in his life that he has ever made public: his contemplation of suicide during World War I. The *New Yorker*, in its turn, recounted another long ago event: "When Jacques Barzun, freshly armed with a Ph.D. in 1932, announced that he intended to write a history of Europe, the di-

---

*I cannot resist noting Barzun's attitude toward acknowledgments, to me a gleam of sanity at a time when the extent of the acknowledgments in most books could readily substitute for the author's biography. No more than I does Barzun see the necessity of thanking everyone with whom one may, from time to time, have discussed one's work. Trilling seems to have concurred in this matter. Barzun records that he and Trilling "read and discussed nearly all of each other's writings in first draft," but neither of them felt impelled publicly to acknowledge this.

rector of the Bibliothèque Nationale took him aside. 'Wait until you're eighty,' he advised the twenty-five-year-old scholar. Barzun thought it over, and thought it over, and then waited until he was nearly ninety to begin."

The *Times* reporter had described the Barzun he saw: "[His] face is leaner and more lined than it once was, his voice is less vigorous, and he walks carefully with a cane. But the only other sign that he is in his 10th decade is that he has accumulated a long lifetime of literary references and historical arguments."

How, having seen him so recently, can I describe him as I knew him in the past, and as I remember after so many years? Oddly enough, his having aged so evidently stunned me less than did the fact that he wore short socks without garters, a sign that for comfort he had eschewed the stricter fashion of a well-dressed man he had followed in earlier years.

No picture of him I have seen, whether rendered by a photographer or by an artist, captures either his physical or his inner qualities. Obvious to the mere observer or the frightened student were his aristocratic way of carrying himself, suggesting arrogance, his impeccable clothes, his neat hair, his studious, exact, but never hesitant speech, his formidable intelligence. I have known history students tempted for the first time in their lives to plagiarize a paper because they could not imagine themselves writing anything that would not affront his critical eye, let alone satisfy him. This was the outer Barzun.

Barzun's description, in his memoir of Trilling, like the customary reaction of students in the Barzun-Trilling seminar to both men, roused me to startled recognition of the Barzun I not only remembered but had later come to know: "Trilling's devotion to his students," Barzun wrote,

> requires the modifier that there were times when he was heartily sick of their presence and their needs and wanted to hide and think like a hermit in a cell. Luckily, it was in the spring that this fit would come on him, whereas my lackluster eye tended to turn

upon the group in autumn. On first acquaintance, Lionel was warmly receptive to the assorted temperaments we had chosen for the year and was immediately popular, while I seemed to them a beast, though possibly a just one. But when his friendly curiosity cooled off, I would become the refuge of the bruised.

(It occurs to me, on rereading Barzun's account of his and Trilling's differing responses to their students, that I have not described Trilling physically as I have described Barzun. Trilling's looks were as famous as his writings, and yet they are not what endure for me. Perhaps it was the chance to glimpse Barzun again that recalled to me the effect of his bodily presence. Trilling has been dead for twenty-five years, and the appearance of a person—as opposed to what they say or induce me to feel—has never stayed with me for long.)

As one came somewhat to know the inner Barzun, nothing of the first, terrifying impression was exactly transfigured. Only now one knew that beneath that stiff exterior he was capable of kindness, attention to others, courtesy of a sort only described by the worn phrase "old-fashioned," and consideration beyond expectation. Without ever meeting Fadiman in the flesh, I suspected him as personally condescending to all but eminent people, and these for the most part men. (This is probably neither fair nor true; I record only a youthful impression.) Trilling I knew to be self-enclosed and harsh to ignorance— not that I blamed him: he would, for example, become annoyed with the umpteenth student to call Wordsworth Wadsworth. Yet, as Barzun put it: "Without really trying, Trilling naturally made disciples" of those young men who responded intelligently to his teachings.

Barzun did not attract disciples in the same way but to my slowly growing amazement, he offered me respect, evident enjoyment in discussing with me our shared enthusiasms, and the courtesy always to reply to the letters, comments, even quotations I had found myself unable to resist sharing with him. His handwriting was, and is, neat, elegant, and completely legible; his comments concise, denoting pleasure.

For example, after the publication of his magnum opus, when he must have been besieged by communications of all sorts, he took the time to send me a clipping from a San Antonio newspaper that, as its quote of the day, had chosen one by me. He also included a statement of mine in his book; nor was he flattering me. He never flattered, and it is true that on the many subjects where we disagreed, he somehow discouraged any attempt I might have made to persuade him of my point of view, or at least to clarify it. Nonetheless, with him I felt as though I had become an acquaintance worth savoring.

Writing the word "acquaintance," I know it to be inaccurate, yet "friendship" serves no better to describe our affiliation; certainly we were never intimate, though when his wife of many years died, he did let me know. I remember the shock of receiving that note, not because of her death—I knew her to be gravely ill—but because he had thought me entitled to know this vital fact. By the 1970s he would inscribe some of his books to me, one "with high esteem and warm regard," the other with "diffidence and affection." I do not imagine that he altogether understood how much this meant to me, but it does certainly suggest that only the youngest of my three male models, and the only one not by birth American, could encourage me as he did. There is no word for our association. To him I was a former student who had turned out to be sufficiently interesting for him not to let me slip away; he treated me with respect and attention. To me, he was a former teacher who, against all expectations arising from his character and mine, seemed at the occasional lunch to find my company satisfactory.

When Michael Murray was chosen by Barzun to be his biographer * —to the astonishment of all that any biographer had been chosen, since "no biography, ever" had seemed to be Barzun's final statement on the matter—Murray came to interview me and admitted that he had so far heard only praise of Barzun, but had been told that I might be the source of negative impressions.

I disabused him, yet I had some idea of how that misapprehen-

---

* Michael Murray, with great generosity, has answered questions and provided me with materials; I am grateful.

sion had come about. Barzun and I had never agreed on politics: he was conservative, at any rate Republican, and I was a Democrat. I can remember him telling me that he knew and liked McGovern—they were fellow historians, he said—but that he could not dream of voting for McGovern as president. He believed that men and women should have separate clubs, which was not altogether fair of him, I thought, since he lunched with me at the Cosmopolitan Club, a woman's club to which at one time I belonged, and to which his dead wife had belonged; her membership, as was the club's policy, was extended to the widower. I could hardly imagine the Century Association extending a membership to a widow. In time, of course, the male exclusiveness of all New York's clubs, including the Century Association, was overcome, to Barzun's regret. (I well remember once being invited by him, as a member of the board of some Columbia publication, to a working dinner at the Century. I was the only woman on the board, and while I was allowed into the club, and even permitted to eat in a private room with the men, I was constantly shadowed, even on my way to the ladies' room, by a watchful employee. It was clear that I might terrorize the members if allowed to wander about.)

Later, after I had met Murray, I learned, but not from him, that another reason I was supposed not to like Barzun was because of May Sarton. I had, in fact, forgotten all about that connection. How odd it is, as one ages, to have bits and pieces of the past thrust upon one and suddenly, like a magnet, gathering to oneself the iron filings of defunct events.

The May Sarton incident revealed itself to my newly stimulated memory as connected to Barzun in two ways. May had always wanted to be embraced by the critical establishment in New York as a writer worthy of their attention, deserving of their honors, and celebrated in their reviews. I tried to explain to her, never with success, that before achieving such distinction, one had to know these eminent literary folks, have dined with them, partied with them, encountered them at various meetings, associations, and celebrations. One might retire to the obscurity of the rural life after achieving a reputation, but one could not achieve it by living always in some small and distant New

England town, regardless of whether one had published estimable books.

This explanation, the truth as I saw it, did not satisfy May. She thought that virtue should be rewarded. Whether she deserved such a reward is a question I do not intend to explore here and did not discuss with her then. Suffice it to say that she wept and wailed at not being taken seriously by the critical elite, above all at not being elected—and this became the chief object of her ambitions—to the American Institute of Arts and Letters. She pleaded with Louise Bogan, the poetry reviewer for the *New Yorker* whom she had long known, to no avail. Saddened by Sarton's misery, I decided to intervene with Barzun on her behalf; an intervention about which she knew nothing. Barzun was twice president of the Academy of Arts and Letters (the Institute's more exclusive arm), although whether he was actually president at that time I do not now remember. He accepted the commission to inquire about the possibility of her being elected, and informed me some time later that he had been told that Sarton was a writer of women's books—this frank condemnation was uttered well before feminism had asserted itself—and that he could do nothing. Perhaps he thought I resented this, although in fact I had undertaken the mission with less than wholeheartedness, not least because I hated to ask favors of this sort, even on behalf of others.

Oddly enough, many years later, I learned from Barzun's second wife, Marguerite, a woman from San Antonio, Texas, that there was a further connection between Barzun and Sarton. We were all dining at the Cosmopolitan Club; I cannot remember what the occasion was, but I had been invited. I asked to be seated—feminism was by now in full throttle, and I had learned to disrupt conventional arrangements, above all at dinner parties—beside Barzun's wife. This was not only from a desire to know her as Barzun's wife but also from a wish to avoid the conversation of a woman's usual dinner-table partner, a dutiful, rarely interesting man. Somehow Marguerite mentioned May Sarton, and went on to tell me that the sister of Barzun's former wife had been a surgeon living in Boston and a lesbian; it was in the latter capacity that she had become a friend of May Sarton. (I learned then, to my intense satisfaction, that the surgeon had left her home in Provence not to Barzun's two sons, as would be the more traditional practice, but to his only daughter, Isabel.) So it turned out that Barzun and Sarton had known each other, or of each other, before I had approached him about Sarton's possible election to the Academy.

Sarton did many years later dine in New York City at the home of Barzun and Marguerite. She reported that she and Barzun had jointly savored their memories of productions of Mozart operas in France in earlier years, but she also reported that he had expressed agreement with Jesse Helms. Since I loathe Jesse Helms and all his acts, I hardly knew what to do with this piece of information, if it was indeed accurate, and decided to ignore it. In any case, these odd concatenations revealed to me why anyone might have thought I disliked Barzun. I could not dislike him, and considered his political views — if indeed they were his political views — in a class with a hatred of dogs or a passionate concern with interior decoration, persuasions dear to some of my closest friends and best ignored. To which it is only fair to add that, whatever his views, Barzun, unlike Trilling, has never been recruited to serve as a grandparent of neoconservativism or of any other ideology.

Barzun retired from Columbia in 1975 — the year Trilling died. Trilling had agreed to write the introduction to the festschrift then being prepared in honor of Barzun's retirement from the university. Never a speedy writer, Trilling, as Diana reported in the festschrift, "was full of fretful impatience because he was coming increasingly to feel that he lacked the strength to get on with a piece he was so eager to write: a recollection of his long years of association with a much-loved friend." Although Trilling was not at that time aware that he was seriously ill, he was, one may guess, blocked at having to encompass so many years, so long a relationship. It is possible — we had heard rumors to this effect — that Trilling and Barzun were no longer so close, no longer in agreement about politics and other matters. But, even if true, that was hardly what was holding Trilling back from completing the introduction at this time. He usually wrote slowly, and wrote now with insufficient energy or health. What stands out for me in the notes he left, however, is this sentence: "It was Jacques who [originally] judged that the distance between him and me might be overcome and who initiated our association."

This practice of "initiating an association" is, I suggest, characteristic of Barzun. Certainly it was he who initiated the relationship between him and me, which I would never have thought of or considered possible. I do not mean, of course, to suggest by this comparison any equivalent significance in his association with Trilling and with me.

The dinner to honor Barzun's retirement and to present him with a festschrift took place in 1976; I cannot remember where the dinner was held, except that it was not at Columbia. I arrived alone, knowing few if any others, and Barzun sat me next to him. There were speeches, which I remember no better than the place. At the end of the ceremony, when the book was presented to Barzun, his thanks for it were punning: "it is not short shrift," he said. I was to learn many years later that, like Fadiman, he relished puns, and at the time I thought this one very clever.

The festschrift volume consisted of essays written to honor Barzun rather than to reflect his particular interests. I had been asked to contribute an essay, either at the suggestion of Barzun himself, or in order to include more essays by women: of the twenty-two essays, four were by women, an impressive number for a Columbia endeavor at that time. The essay I wrote was hardly likely to appeal to Barzun; I had, however, already learned about the latitude he offered to longtime acquaintances. My essay dealt with the disability of the female imagination—that is, the inability of female authors to present authentic women protagonists or, as we say, heroes—in the works of many writers. This disability was, I demonstrated, particularly evident in the work of the popular novelist Mary Renault. Contributors to the festschrift were also asked to include a quotation from Barzun at the head of our essays. Mine read: "Stendhal would very likely say that woman should be brilliant if unable to be beautiful," from *The Energies of Art*. We were also asked to provide our own contributor's biography, written in the third person, and I wrote that Heilbrun's "recent publication, *Towards a Recognition of Androgyny*, while counter to most Barzun inclinations, received his support, as its author had always enjoyed his encouragement." I went on to discuss the many enthusiasms we shared, including detective fiction.

We had discussed detective novels for almost ten years before I told Barzun that I was Amanda Cross. I had begun writing in secret, and maintained silence about my authorship for most of that time. But one day Barzun asked me if I had any idea who Amanda Cross was, and in reply to that direct question I told him she was I. His astonishment was satisfactory indeed. I had never before — and would never again — see him dumbfounded. Mine were not the sort of mysteries he especially admired, but he was kind enough to include my first detective novel among his selection of later detective fiction, *A Catalogue of Crime*. In this book he kept my secret, except for what I called his hanky-panky in the index, where I was listed both pseudonymously and by my real name.

It is no wonder that Barzun liked my first detective novel best, for while in later books Kate Fansler, my detective, became more feminist and more radical, if only mildly so, in that first adventure she was unconventional only in being female. Obviously influenced by Sayers, *In the Last Analysis* was unusual for the time in having a woman sleuth — as I have noted, only Agatha Christie's Miss Marple was also in print at the time. Writing in 1963, the year of *The Feminine Mystique*, I hardly dared to give my protagonist more than an independent life: she was a professional, she was rich, attractive, with sexual experience, and no wish to marry — eccentric enough at the period, but not so far out as to displease the conventional reader — and, alas, certainly not feminist.

Not that Barzun was conventional about women's role — certainly he was less so than Fadiman or Trilling, and less likely to swipe at women if opportunity offered — but he was deeply devoted to the strictest interpretation of detective fiction, one which I would, in ensuing books, leave far behind. The series Fifty Classics of Crime Fiction (1971) that Barzun edited with Wendell Hertig Taylor included American and English detective novels published between 1900 and

1950. The one volume of stories, the first of the fifty classics, seems to me now hopelessly dated (and only one of the stories was by a woman). Of the novels published in the series, however, nine were by women—reflecting the fact that women writers were a major element in what is called "the golden age" of detective fiction, referring to the novels written in England between the wars. All fifty of these classics were qualified to be considered the best of their time, and they were books I had read and reread with pleasure. But they all, even those by women, featured a restricted, upper class world of educated, privileged white men. Above all, these novels and stories were true renditions of detection—the solving of a crime through attention to complex material clues.

As Barzun put it in his essay "Detective and Fiction," in *The Energies of Art*, "it would be foolish to deny that detection in literature submits to very rigid canons." For him, detective stories are not novels but tales: that is, an ancient form of puzzle where the protagonist performs "three impossible tasks before morning." Most important, detective fiction must concern itself with physical objects, not with mental states; the reader of this fiction must be eager to explore "the nature and connections of the inanimate—including the corpse." In happy contemplation of these inanimate objects, Barzun and his ideal reader must be ready "to swallow long descriptions of houses and their furnishings, [be] greedy for the contents of posthumous pockets, [and] long to master time tables, speeds of vehicles, and procedures for collecting evidence."

What this form of fiction must, above all, abjure are "stories of anxiety," which Barzun goes so far as to call "self-abuse." Scorning the marriage of detective fiction with other forms, Barzun is stern: "The novelist's hero may agonize through an 'identity crisis' or uncover the sinister forces that make for social injustice, but the bedeviled figures in crime fiction labor under more urgent needs"—that is, finding out who done it and how.

As with so much of Barzun's yearning for a more neatly delineated past, where art was art, detection was detection, and personal agony or social anger had no place in either, this hope too, for what he saw as the exemplary form of detective fiction, was to remain unsatisfied. More and more as the second half of the century unfolded, the mystery story came to resemble the novel, and indeed was more likely than the majority of mainstream fiction to venture upon courageous innovations. Women detectives seemed to increase exponentially, and by the beginning of this twenty-first century, there are detectives of many ethnic origins, all acutely aware of their place in the world and the suffering involved in being there.

My own theories about crime novels have developed far beyond what Barzun would then, or possibly will yet, allow. Indeed, I credit the contemporary detective fiction featuring women sleuths with an extraordinary accomplishment, and I am, in fact, convinced that the first genuine woman hero, not previously depicted, may be found incarnated as the contemporary female detective in fiction—though I fear this assertion would disturb Barzun. I believe that, starting in the late 1960s, women detectives who were neither conventional nor committed to the safe and sure began to emerge in mystery narratives. Women detectives had been imagined before; but it was not until the list of books in print included more women sleuths than one could easily count that a revolution had arrived. Like all women's revolutions, it has been little noticed, and noticed by the media only to be scorned. Not perfection; not even comfort, or acclamation, or absolute success mark the careers of these intrepid women and their creators. But there they are, for the first time in literature: female protagonists who do not conform to any female pattern yet devised, inscribed, or recommended.

Why, it might be asked, has no one, even those less rigid than Barzun in describing the genre, recognized them for the miracle they are —"miracle" in the sense of something not before imagined? Considering the degree to which the contemporary female detective scorns the dictates of custom, history, and the earlier restrictions of womanhood, it is remarkable that her unique destiny has been largely unnoticed and even more rarely commented upon. The reason, of course, is because she has appeared in popular fiction. (How Barzun might cringe at that term.)

Geniuses, I now long to propose to Barzun (if only he hadn't moved to Texas), including those yet to emerge in the twenty-first century, do not spring from nowhere to dazzle us with their perfection. The way is cleared for geniuses, whether in music, or literature, or art, by less astonishingly gifted creators who take the chances, try out the new, and leave behind works deeply flawed and oddly original. They never achieve the magnificence, the style, the elegance of those who will eventually follow them, but they are as essential to the production of geniuses as they are often ignored or disdained. If feminist detective novels will never win a mainstream prize, one day such a prize will be won by a writer who learned from these stories how to imagine a female protagonist in no way ready to settle for love, or domesticity, or submission, or the ancient lure of coupledom. Few, even including the perspicacious Barzun, will be likely to guess in what context this creature was born, any more than those who relish a performance of Hamlet are aware that without Kyd's popular revenge tragedies we would have had no Shakespeare. As, in a more feminist mode, we now know how few have recognized that Jane Austen's extraordinary fictions — alone, of all women writers, admired by almost all manly men — would not have been possible without the many less gifted women novelists who preceded her and whom she devoured with such delight.

In short, Barzun's admired kind of crime fiction has evolved, to my satisfaction and, I assume, to his regret, into a new and vital form that does, alas, allow for the exploration of "the sinister forces that make for social injustice." To which it is only fair to add that Barzun and I both denigrate the American macho detective story exemplified by Raymond Chandler, who, having been educated in England and admitting to English tastes, should not have taken the American detective novel so far along the path of senseless violence.

Ah, well. Trilling taught me the literary force of "in betweenness" and Fadiman the appeal of criticism available to the nonacademic intelligent reader; they both did so, however, in words that excluded women from their high ideals. Barzun, on the other hand, did not scorn or denigrate the writings of women. He included among his original fifty classic detective novels, for example, *The Division Bell Mystery*, by Ellen Wilkinson, a union organizer, Labour MP, ardent feminist, and a reforming Minister of Education until her too early death in 1947. Her novel is certainly detective fiction of the sort dear to Barzun's heart, but her political alliances and radical views, which peek through her fiction, did not dissuade him from including her novel in his series. Certainly she does not commit the ultimate sin against the genre: her work is emphatically not "devoid of detection" or physical detail.

Thus matters stood in 1971, when *A Catalogue of Crime* was first published. When the new edition was published in 1989, it bore a new "introductory," testifying to the fact that Barzun had stayed abreast of crime writing events (I have always assumed, with apologies to Taylor, that Barzun wrote these introductions; they are in his style and sound like him). Not that he was confessing to a turnabout, but he was ready to declare that "the attitude of the reading public to crime fiction has radically altered." And indeed it had. Now, observing that the pleasure of reading crime fiction was intellectual, he was widening his definition of this genre's rewards beyond the clever solving of cases. Since it has long been my view that the writers of detective novels, if not always the detectives, are invariably highly educated, I was glad to see this broader outlook.

Barzun is still hard on women: they excel in crime fiction because domesticity has taught them to attend to detail, but, as a corollary, too "many stories by women consist of nothing but trivial matters of which nothing is made. The writers lack organizing power—the sense of relevance and the imagination to infer conclusions from scattered facts." This is doubtless true, but it is equally true of male-authored novels: the trivia are, however, of a different sort—and, as we all know, nothing men do is considered trivia. Barzun repeats that a work of crime fiction is never a great novel, which may be correct, although as I have argued, it may lead to great novels. Barzun's wit, meanwhile, is right on target and suggests a certain loosening of his rigid definitions: "we can accept a private eye who thinks about political corruption and the vices of the rich, and who is keen about jazz; but when he drinks and fornicates incessantly we cease to believe in his capacity for consecutive thought."

And here, in his introduction to *A Catalogue of Crime*, Barzun is not only acclaiming the work of women writers but actually inquiring where they have been since the days of his youth. "It is odd that fictional women—and but a few at that [Really, Professor Barzun, and in 1989!]—have only begun to take their share of this burden; or rather, to take it up again for at the turn of the last century, when feminism reached a high point, the 'female detective' was popular and ubiquitous." If this is not quite sound history, it at least recognizes the recurring connection between women detectives and feminism, and offers solace for previous slights. And for this solace I am grateful.

But of course his major interest was never detective fiction, but art in all its highest forms. And he had very definite views on the decline of this art in the last half of the twentieth century.

Jacques Barzun II

That the contemporary world—since 1920—
has merely amplified and multiplied what the nineties and
early 1900s first achieved, I must ask you to take on faith.
We lack the time here to survey the whole evidence,
which is overwhelming.

JACQUES BARZUN, *Mellon Lecture*

BARZUN'S DEVOTION to the form of crime fiction in earlier times marks an allegiance to art in general; his disinclination to admire or even tolerate art of the last half of the twentieth century is emphatic, and in sharp contrast to his elegant, wittily written appreciations of earlier times. When Barzun wishes there to be no "sinister forces that make for social injustice," he is pleading for a refusal of the personal, the political, the revolutionary in all art. Similarly, in his memoir of Trilling—full of appreciation and decorum, with emotion evident beneath the words—Barzun never mentions the most fundamental and continuous influence on Trilling's life: the fact that he was a Jew. As Trilling wrote in his journal, "Being a Jew is like walking in the wind or swimming: you are touched at all points and conscious everywhere." It is, of course, possible, even likely, that Trilling never spoke to the gentile Barzun about being Jewish.

Nevertheless, Barzun's dislike of sloppy, personal suffering making its way into art is palpable. Not that he would for a moment encourage Faulkner's sentiment, one Barzun quoted in his 1973 Mellon lecture, *The Use and Abuse of Art*: "If a writer has to rob his mother, he will not hesitate: the 'Ode on a Grecian Urn' is worth any number of old ladies"—a sentiment, however, Barzun adds that "many people would applaud without scruple." It is perhaps the egoism of contemporary writers that rouses Barzun to disdain—and not, one must admit, without reason. Yet he also tells the lecture audience that he will "be dealing with art as a single force in modern life." The word "modern," in this context, means "contemporary," although for Barzun, as for all historians, the modern period begins with the Renaissance. And as Barzun contemplates our world, he asserts that "Western civilization has not had a new idea in fifty years." Since he was speaking in 1973, therefore the last time art may be said to have actually been created must, in his opinion, be 1923.

The period Barzun really means to identify as the source of all that is commendable in this century's art encompasses the years between 1890 and World War I. Barzun was born in 1907, into the flourishing art of those years, and it is the only period of his life he speaks of many times in a personal tone. World War I, he writes, "flung its men into the trenches, visibly destroyed that nursery of living culture. Work ceased, conversation dulled, relatives and friends vanished." He paints the world he was born into for the lecture audience:

> I grew up in Paris before World War I, and not merely in the atmosphere of the new art of the century, but in the very midst of its creation. As a child in my father's house I was surrounded by the young poets, painters, musicians, and sculptors who made Cubism, concrete poetry, atonality and the rest. Varèse, Apollinaire, Ezra Pound, Léger, Gleizes, Severini, Villon, Duchamp, Duchamp-Villon, Marie Laurencin, Cocteau and many others were to me household names in the literal sense—names of familiar figures around the house.

And he did add, in his friend Clifton Fadiman's collection *Living Philosophies*, his unique account of personal suffering:

> The outbreak of war in August 1914 and the nightmare that ensued put an end to all innocent joys and assumptions. . . . Throughout, poisoning all other sentiments, was the continual outpouring of public hatred. By the age of ten—I was later told—my words and attitudes betrayed suicidal thoughts; it appeared that I was "ashamed" to be alive. Steps were taken: before the

end of the school term in 1918 I was bundled off to the seashore, away from "events," including the bombardment of Paris.

Barzun goes on to tell us how

> with beach life and surrender to a great lassitude, calm slowly returned, helped out by reading adventure stories. But it was not Gulliver and Robinson Crusoe alone who restored the will to live; it was also Hamlet. I had taken him off the shelf in Paris, not in secret but unnoticed, and I brought him away with me. . . . Especially comforting was his ability to overcome his doubts in the terrible murkiness of his situation. . . . Fortinbras said what a good king he would have made "had he been put on." Thus were the trials of my young life made coherent in a view of Hamlet I have never found reason to alter.

The portrait Barzun paints of his idyllic childhood before the war holds a particular significance for me: I have noticed that those with happy early childhoods will often be reluctant to consider the present or future as worthy of that past time.

Nor, understandably, has he ever found reason to alter his view of the power and originality of those years as compared with all that followed. His thesis in all he wrote, including his latest book, *From Dawn to Decadence*, would always be that nothing accomplished by generations who were not adults at the time of World War I was either original or, if original, worthy.

Barzun's longest and most impressive account of this thesis is in the introduction to *The Energies of Art*, 1956, an article version of which he sent me in 1966, before I had any idea of his views on the disaster of World War I. I had received a Guggenheim fellowship to write a book on what I called, being rooted in English rather than French literature, *The Edwardian Years*. I had discovered, hardly originally, that all the great new ideas of the twentieth century, in science, music, dance, medicine, as well as art, had been established in the years around the turn of the century, and destroyed by the war. It was my view that not until the 1960s did our century catch up with what had earlier been accomplished. Barzun's article, the copy he sent encouragingly inscribed to me, confirmed my ideas.

In the event I did not write that book, having read my way through all I could find on Edwardian England—a period I arbitrarily extended from 1910 to 1914—only to become interested in another idea of that period: the changing boundaries of gender and the revival of the ancient concept of androgyny. I am sure Barzun thought this switch regrettable. I sent him my 1973 book on androgyny, which he did not care for, but praised as best he could by observing—he was right—that the section on Bloomsbury, a group not so often discussed at that time, was the most persuasive.

It is hardly to be wondered at that for Barzun art ended with the destruction of his childhood world. Nor do I disagree that the root of most modern concepts originated before World War I. What I find troubling, however, is Barzun's double-edged assault on all art since. On the one hand, if a work of literature is commendable, he insists that its ideas were certainly established and perhaps better stated by writers between the Victorian age and the war. On the other hand, he chooses the most extreme and terrible works to exemplify the horrors of contemporary art.

For example, to illustrate the first of these points—that "the contemporary world has, since 1920, merely amplified and multiplied what the nineties and early 1900s first achieved," he snarls at Roger Fry, Clive Bell, and their concept of "significant form. Do not ask," he quips, "significant of what?" Not only is this snarl unworthy, but Barzun fails to contemplate the affecting scene in Virginia Woolf's *To the Lighthouse* where Mr. Bankes stares in wonder at Lily Briscoe's painting of Mrs. Ramsay and her child:

> Taking out a pen-knife, Mr. Bankes tapped the canvas with the bone handle. What did she wish to indicate by the triangular purple shape, "just there"? he asked.
>
> It was Mrs. Ramsay reading to James, she said. She knew his objection—that no one could tell it for a human shape. But she had made no attempt at likeness, she said. For what reason had

she introduced them then? he asked. Why indeed?—except that in there, in that corner, it was bright, here, in this, she felt the need of darkness. . . . Mr. Bankes was interested. Mother and child then—objects of universal veneration, and in this case the mother was famous for her beauty—might be reduced, he pondered, to a purple shadow without irreverence.

But the picture was not of them, she said. Or not in his sense. There were other senses too in which one might reverence them. By a shadow here and a light there, for instance. . . . A mother and child might be reduced to a shadow without irreverence.

Mr. Bankes, in this conversation, has always seemed to me, in his questions, to resemble Barzun, except perhaps that Mr. Bankes is slightly more willing to try to appreciate this new theory of art. For it is a fact that significant form was a new and important idea, one that enabled Roger Fry to change England's ideas about art and to introduce the postimpressionists into Britain's culture.

To illustrate Barzun's other major thesis, his repulsion from contemporary art, he offers an egregious example:

Consider an English play of the mid-sixties entitled *Saved*, in which occurs a scene that attracted a great deal of attention when produced. A baby wheeled in a pram in a London park becomes the butt of several adult hoodlums, who egg each other on to badger the infant, who then roll it about in its own excretions, and finally kill it by hurling stones at it while one man urges the others to urinate on it. In an interview with the press the producer congratulated himself on having won the right to stage a scene of such originality and significance.

By using such examples, Barzun makes it difficult for anyone to disagree with him when he declares that, in the light of certain of the less palatable moments of contemporary art, "what we are witnessing in all the arts and in all that the arts refer to, is the liquidation of 500 years of civilization—the entire modern age dating from the Renaissance." Yet to leap from Shakespeare, as an example of the glories of the Renaissance, to *Saved*, as the example of 500 years of decadence, seems a bit out of balance. This, nonetheless, will be the theme of *From Dawn to Decadence*.

Never scornful of women, and uninterested in questions of gender, Barzun in *From Dawn to Decadence* pays attention and deference to many prominent women. But that the changing concept of what culture demands of women might be new, invigorating, or challenging is not to him a viable idea. Thus he considers inversion of the sexes in theatrical productions as a device used only to "activate the classics," not to reenvision them or question sex roles. "Since Euripides' *Trojan Women* has chief roles for women only," he laments, "let us give it with an all-male cast. Even more 'interesting' by virtue of greater confusion is to use an all-male cast for *Antony and Cleopatra*." That new light might be shed on classic plays that were written only for men in all the roles does not carry weight with Barzun.

"What is the essence of one's own time?" Barzun asks and answers: "Revolution, reaction, retreat, escape, indifference." As my disquisition on detective fiction testifies, I think the essence of one's own time may quite properly be the transformation of hitherto universally accepted ideas. Barzun, without intending it, expresses my view when he says: "the tide turns, and like those of the ocean, the tides of culture are an obscure phenomenon under the protection of luna, the moon." He and I disagree only over "what in the course of a work of rehabilitation has seemed significant." Clearly for me, as for Diana Trilling, the changed status of women is the primary revolution of our time.

If Barzun seems to me sadly unappreciative of contemporary art and culture, he is marvelously correct in matters of teaching. The year 2000 saw the publication of Diane Ravitch's *Left Back: A Century of Failed School Reforms*, a book that postulates almost every criticism and suggestion that Barzun urged in *Teacher in America* in 1945; like Barzun, Ravitch understands that when the schools undertook to promote social and personal goals, they ceased effectively to educate the children in what needed to be learned. Yet Ravitch does not mention Barzun's work and may not even have heard of it. The essence of our time does seem too often to require the repetition of wisdom already promulgated and examined. Had Ravitch noted Barzun's observations decades earlier, she might have better understood the recalcitrance of the conditions both he and she are describing.

In the days before Trilling's death, when he sat down to try to compose his tribute to Barzun, he had on his desk two of Barzun's books: *The Energies of Art* and *Teacher in America*. Trilling probably was more in agreement than I with Barzun's views on contemporary art, but when it came to recognizing the scope of Barzun's achievement, he selected the same two books to represent that scope that I, so many years later, have chosen to discuss here. To these works, Trilling might have added Barzun's writings on music, particularly his biography of Berlioz. Indeed, though *The Energies of Art* does discuss music, I may as well admit that my favorite Barzun flourishes not only in the Berlioz biography but, even more endearingly, in *A Stroll with William James* (1983). Barzun is, in my view, a scintillating, intelligent biographer, and it is in his evaluation of William James's life and work that Barzun best exemplifies, for me, his unique talents.

Barzun categorizes *A Stroll with William James* as "the record of an intellectual debt. If," he adds, "it gives pleasure or knowledge, I shall be glad"; Barzun's book gave me both, although, or perhaps because, I had been an admirer of William James for many years. "Admirer," is an insufficient word; Barzun more accurately enunciates my reaction to James's work: "his words, his temperament speak to me with intimacy as well as force. Communication is direct; I do not 'derive benefit' from him, he 'does me good.'"

Barzun discusses James's pragmatism, his religious views, above all his definition of generosity: "James's simple idea that the burden of proof in our moral relations is always on the negative: given a claim concretely presented, why should I not satisfy it. The search for a 'why should I?' is futile see-sawing." This clarification has long sustained me. Above all, Barzun knows that James was unique as a philosopher; he alone did not reject, indeed supported, the "notion of duty to the common world of ideas." Contemporary philosophers tended to deal with narrow linguistic matters, unintelligible and uninteresting to the educated nonspecialist. James, I have often thought, may well have suffered from writing too clearly, by avoiding strict theories, by understanding that it is only when one writes precisely what one means that one discovers what one means.

Barzun also offers an excellent analysis of pragmatism, together with a refutation of all the nonsense that has accumulated around the concept. I became a pragmatist when I first read James, and have remained one. Pragmatism encourages concreteness of thought; as Barzun puts it, pragmatism is not a philosophy, "it is an attempt to explain how the mind ascertains truth" and to account for the variability of truth. As Barzun phrases James's theme: "Go and see if experience responds; find out if later perceptions . . . bear out the interpretation. . . . Note also whether the new idea fits in with earlier accepted ones." Here again, Barzun considers the contemporary world a mere matter of repetition, chaos, and despair. He therefore identifies James as "an existential thinker: that is, one who philosophizes from the need to survive intellectually and emotionally in a universe that the collapse of traditional religion and the tyranny of science have laid waste."

On religion, Barzun, selecting James's phrases, identified for me and for all those with religious impulses but with disaffection with organized religion, prescribed forms of worship, or reliance on an infinite power, the quality of spiritual consciousness: "'Something larger than ourselves perhaps only a larger and more godlike self,' but at any rate 'beyond each man a larger power which is friendly to him— only so much is needed to give the individual comfort and spur him to bend his energies in that same direction. For most men do require a centering purpose and for many it must be transcendent.'"

We note here James's use of the male noun and pronoun. Barzun, writing in 1983, and sensitive to questions of gender and sex roles, although he claims to find "vagueness" in the terms "racism" and "sexism," devotes ample attention to the question of women and their relation to James—both women generally and the women in James's life. Here, as he will in *From Dawn to Decadence*, Barzun declares that the word "Man" means "human beings, in keeping with etymology";

he also replaces the usual "he" with the phrase "he and she." Most significantly for my purposes, Barzun goes out of his way to describe and, if truth be told, defend James's relation to his wife—named Alice, like the sister of William and Henry. Barzun's depiction of wife Alice serves as a portrait of his own ideal of a highly satisfactory companion to an unusually gifted man. "It was not merely that she made a home for him, became his amanuensis, and protected him from unwelcome intrusions; . . . the greater part of what he wrote to her consisted of social, moral, and philosophical observations that plainly show the companion she was on the plane of intellect. . . . William now had a collaborator in the literal sense of the term."

And, be it also noted, the ideal companion need not be beautiful, particularly if she has spent considerable time in Germany, learned to speak German fluently and studied the piano with Clara Schumann: "William did not look like a matinee idol. Alice was twenty-seven years old, stocky, and only her eyes, in a face without delicate features, revealed her intelligence, character, and vitality. These, of course, and her wit, appeared in her talk, uttered in a resonant, well-modulated voice that hearers noticed and did not forget." Nice, I thought, except for the "well-modulated voice," which evokes Lear's encomium on Cordelia, a phrase emblazoned in my day at the entrance to the Wellesley Library: "Her voice was ever soft, gentle and low, an excellent thing in woman." This was an admonition that profoundly annoyed me at the time; today I think it marvelously inappropriate: the Wellesley girls of my day should, rather, have been told to rage, rage against almost everything. One also rather regrets that "Alice's secretarial help became indispensable in dealing with his ever enlarging correspondence."

But it is in the matter of James's odd, indeed puzzling desertion of Alice and his first child at the birth of their second son that Barzun reveals his idea that childbirth within a happy marriage is an exclusively maternal undertaking. William was away for six months from just before his baby's arrival, making the rounds of the intellectual centers of Europe. That his father also died in America during this period is perhaps irrelevant. But surely one has to question the impulses that drive a man so far, and for so long, from the occasion of birth. Without in any sense denying Barzun's distaste for the endless psychologizing of biographers, it does appear evident that this is, for a man of William's kindness and profound sense of moral obligation, eccentric and compulsive behavior. Barzun disagrees: "Alice was expecting a second child and he knew that leaving her, in excellent health and with her mother close by, to deal alone with the birth and the necessary recasting of domestic arrangements, would be a relief to her. She thought him clumsy and useless around the house, and the very depth and force of his sympathy could be trying." Does not Barzun's defense of William in this case suggest an inclination toward the same behavior on his own part? What other explanation seems plausible? Yet who can disagree with Barzun's delightful insight about offspring? "Except by chance, it seems there is no way to bring up children right—though some ways may be a little better than others."

Barzun's insistence that nothing has occurred after 1920 that was not set fully in motion in the decades before turns up even in *A Stroll with William James*. In mentioning what he calls "the battle for women's rights," he asserts that the battle had indeed begun before World War I. To this assertion, he adds a footnote:

"Battle" is not a metaphor, nor was sexual emancipation merely a program. The best souls gave lectures on birth control and practiced free love on principle, marriage and domesticity being evident forms of slavery. In pursuit of the vote, well-bred women turned into demonic street orators, stormed government buildings and initiated the sit-in, invaded Parliament, and after bloody scuffles with the police went triumphantly to jail. Poor Augustine Birrell, a literary man who was also an M.P., was knocked down and trampled by five women in St. James Park. Other suffragettes took up revolver practice and one martyr threw herself under the racing horses at Ascot.

One may be forgiven for inferring that Barzun's view of these activities was not entirely benign. Indeed, although he is so far ahead of Fadiman or Trilling in his attempts to meet the requirements of changing sexual mores, his requirements for the satisfactory woman still position a man as the center of her orbit if she is to be deemed both rational and sufficiently attractive.

Despite this male-centric attitude, Barzun always took the opportunity to admire accomplished women—from the medieval period to the time of William James. We may glance back to his appreciation and defense in *Race: A Study in Superstition*, 1937, of even those frequently sneered at:

> As the daughter of the Swiss Financier and Statesman Necker, the future Madame de Staël had been reared among the most cultured Parisian circle of the old regime. Her marriage at twenty with the German diplomat, the Baron de Staël-Holstein, and her unacceptable political views during the later Revolution, Consulate, and Empire increased her opportunities of travel outside France. She therefore was by taste and circumstance at the opposite pole from narrow nationalism. Indeed the main purpose of her two great books—*Literature Considered in Its Relation to Society*, 1800, and *De l'Allemagne*, 1810—was not to foster race-theories but to introduce the new Germany of Kant, Goethe, and Schiller to the French. This remains her great achievement despite cavil from nationalist critics on both sides of the Rhine. . . . Until one reads her books one can hardly imagine the cultural chasm she was trying to span.

Since Madame de Staël has seldom been given the credit due her—for example for introducing German romanticism into England—that Barzun was able to appreciate this influential, though hardly beautiful woman, is particularly rewarding.

But to return from that byway to *A Stroll with William James*. My response to so satisfactory a book is, for the most part, a happy wallow in admiration for both James and the manner in which Barzun has evoked him. James, for instance, is perfect on my favorite occupation, one that appears to me to be the epitome of intense and lasting human pleasure: conversation. James, like Barzun, understood its major elements; Barzun had the gift of it. In *Any Number Can Play*, 1957, Fadiman told of a radio program that, in those less ad-driven times, he had been able to organize: "A couple of years ago a small group of professional communicators, myself among them, contrived to smuggle onto the airwaves a radio program called *Conversation*." Discussing the participants in that program, Fadiman rated Barzun highly: "The best talker the program has developed, in my opinion, is an academically trained historian with a European background. He is used to judging experience rather than exchanging experiences; comparing ideas rather than personal tastes; and striking from his contemplation of character rather than from his recollection of the gossip column."

And here is Barzun quoting James on conversation: "When two minds of high order, interested in kindred subjects, come together, their conversation is chiefly remarkable for the summariness of its allusions and the rapidity of its transitions." James was even better at complaining of nonconversation, though he restricted this description to a private letter: "I've been meeting minds so earnest and helpless that it takes them half an hour to get from one idea to its immediately adjacent next neighbor. And then they lie down on it with their whole weight and can get no farther, like a cow on a doormat, so that you can get neither in nor out with them."

Because we shared "kindred subjects," Jacques Barzun and I occasionally enjoyed, over the years, what I like to remember as good conversation. What I certainly recall with exactness is the kind of impersonal companionship I shared with him, a companionship unique in my experience. He and I, as I have earlier remarked, were never intimate—it is unclear that intimacy would be Barzun's chosen mode with anyone, even had I been, as was hardly to be expected, the likely recipient of such a privilege. Yet, because of this impersonal companionship, he allowed me to imagine that what had earlier seemed an unattainable "male" vocation—such as he and Fadiman and Trilling represented—would not be forever absolutely denied to me.

And though we held differing opinions on many subjects, including detective fiction, he encouraged me in my endeavors. Recently, I discovered the extent of his past generosity. My publisher had decided to furnish new covers for my paperback mysteries, and sent me examples of these. The cover for *Poetic Justice* now bore on its face a blurb Barzun had provided for the original publication in 1972. I had forgotten about it; so, no doubt, had he. I would guess that, because of the great success of *From Dawn to Decadence*, Barzun's words had been revived.

Their appearance on the front of my old book startled me yet again into a recognition of his remarkable good will toward one who, upon first encountering him, could not have imagined the possibility of any such outcome. Of the three men who taught me so much, Barzun alone served not only as an example of how one might think and write and speak. He was also the only one of the three who reached across the abyss that divided us—Fadiman I never met and Trilling proffered not even slight support—to tender something close to friendship as well as encouragement.

EPILOGUE

I am much nearer [their] age now than my own then.
But do I therefore "understand" [them] better than I did?
Or have I only queered the angle of that immensely important
relationship, so that I shall fail to describe it, either from [their]
point of view or my own? I see [them] now from round
the corner; not directly in front of me.
VIRGINIA WOOLF, "A Sketch of the Past"

———

LOOKING BACK to half a century ago and at the years that followed, what was it these three men offered that has felt so significant to me in subsequent times? Feminism has intervened; the inevitable limits of these three men's world and imagination in regard to women have become evident. I have the sense of having been rescued, by feminism, from the rejection and heartbreak that my life might have been had I attempted to follow in the path of these three men, and attempted to win their commendation. Yet the power they held over me does not seem less significant now, as I might expect it would. Why is that?

To dream of a life, to fantasize a life, is certainly easier than to live it. I have said elsewhere that it is harder to write of a new way of life than to live it. George Eliot is a prime example: she never offers her heroines the life she so bravely achieved. But I speak here of fantasy, not of practical dreams or revolution. Unrealistic fantasy explains why so many novels in the past ended with wedding bells. The marriage did not have to be endured by readers, only by the participants, and then it was not to be overseen. Hope was all that mattered, that and the experience, at least in novels, of "being in love." I think of Anne Eliot in *Persuasion*, happy at last with her lost love returned to her. The movie ends with the couple on his ship, but the book does not. Unlike Admiral Croft, Wentworth does not believe in women on ships; Anne's will not be the happy maritime companionship of the Crofts.

She will wait at home, as the novel tells us, for years at a time. A war looms. She will have children, and spend many years alone with them. The love she was faithful to will, upon its consummation, become a distant love, full of perils. But we are not required to participate in that aspect of her life.

I was not told that, having been given my wished-for opportunity to become a colleague of Trilling's and Barzun's at Columbia (just as Anne Eliot was given her longed-for chance to marry Wentworth), I would suffer a new isolation. Nor did I further guess that, enabled because of feminism to achieve a professorship without denying my sex or my woman's way of interpretation, I would meet with new troubles, new failures, new disappointments. The early years of feminism were, like all early loves, passionate, erotic, invigorating, full of possibility. Then the problems that life inevitably brings set in. I would not trade a moment of it for all the romance in the world, but it was certainly fraught with anxiety, battles, betrayals, and failures as well as with accomplishment. What matters, of course, is that it was life—a life I had chosen and not permitted to be chosen for me.

The three men, meanwhile, remain in my imagination still as the object of my hopes, as a lovely dream that satisfied some of my longings, and was not required to fulfill the other yearnings—as indeed it could not. Like the perfection of the man one did not marry, of the life one did not choose, of the child one did not have, the dream remains unchallenged by reality. I still think of those three men as perfect in the hour when I first saw them, first recognized them, first transformed them into my models and my pattern of the intellectual life.

Looking back upon them is to be transported to another world. Reading about them since those first years has once again made me understand that men cannot, ultimately, offer women complete patterns for their lives. When, as in the case of Mary McCarthy and Hannah Arendt, such an offer seems to be accepted, it is because the women are allotted a place in groups of men that is uniquely theirs, a tribute to their special attractions, and not a place where other women may follow. When I read today of Susan Sontag's scorn for Lionel Trilling and his kind of criticism, I respond with the recognition that for all his misogyny and pomposity, Trilling still represents an important kind of honor that I seem to miss today. He had the courage not to entice his readers into admiring his erudition but to make plain with clarity his ideas and how he arrived at them: these ideas were often complex, but his rendition of them was not. Unlike Sontag, he placed popular culture in context, often in opposition to literature, but he did not do so in the hope of dazzling his readers. Rather, he wished to take them along with him into the intricacies of the intellectual life lived, or endured, in a culture compounded of anxieties, in a consumer society of dubious values.

Wendy Lesser tells us that as an undergraduate, she was not very fond of Wordsworth; she read him "as merely assigned reading." When she returned, some four decades later to Wordsworth's Immortality Ode, it was through Lionel Trilling's essay on Wordsworth's poem in his *The Liberal Imagination*.

Unlike those conservatives today who believe that Trilling would have agreed with them, unlike Sontag who set out to surpass his kind of criticism, unlike me, who can no longer find anything new or sustaining in the writings I had almost memorized a half century ago, Lesser, realizing that she had not read Trilling's book as an undergraduate, writes today:

> I thought I had [read it], because its author and title were so much a part of the academic air I breathed in my youth; Trilling's book had been valued by most of the people who taught me. But when I picked it up to reread it, I discovered it was practically all new to me. And what a discovery it was. My first response was an almost paralyzing admiration: why had anyone bothered to write literary criticism after Lionel Trilling, when he had already said everything worth saying? And even when I calmed down a bit— enough to see there were perhaps a few dark corners his wise clearsightedness had left unclarified—I remained filled with enormous respect for his enterprise. He was speaking about

things that mattered in a voice that presumed his readership cared about such things, and the strength of that assurance, in the face of the four subsequent decades experience to the contrary, powerfully bolstered me. This was literary criticism I could learn from.

What I think this so recent judgment of Trilling's work testifies to is his enduring gift for inspiring with its essential magic a piece of literature only seriously engaged with for the first time. To enter upon the study of any writing, and to see it through Trilling's eyes, is to learn what literature can be, to begin to perceive its infinite complexity.

If Trilling developed an "image," it was not one he contrived, and indeed it caused him significant distress when he recognized its strength and its implications. The same might be said of Fadiman and Barzun. David Brooks may find them overdoing their defense of intellect, too ardently urging, in plain prose, the power and importance of intellect, but I am glad to have learned that way of living and writing rather than the media-mad, antiintellectual way of confronting the world of today. I had learned from these three men that to be unpopular is not death, that to be famous may indeed be a form of annihilation, and that there is never, ever, a resting place. I am glad enough to live in today's culture, I do not condemn it, but like all cultures it has been bought at the price of much that I cherish—clarity of language and expression above all. That may seem to make me, as all old people are supposed to be, old-fashioned, worshipping the past, but this is not the case: I am far more radical about the condition of women in our world than Sontag or McCarthy or Arendt would have dared or chosen to be. (Characteristically, Arendt wrote to William Phillips who had met Simone de Beauvoir, "The trouble with you, William, is that you don't realize that she's not very bright. Instead of arguing with her, you should flirt with her.")

They were for me a moment in time, these three men, however long they lived beyond that moment. I have followed them into their later years because of the great consequences they had in my life and my aspirations, and because I wondered how they had changed, compared to the transformations I had undergone since encountering them. I found that they were as I remembered them, that they still inspired my admiration and amazement, even if their later works were not always, in my view, of equal merit to their earlier more youthful endeavors. Barzun alone of the three, while he did not change his dire opinions of the twentieth century's last seventy years, continued productively to engage, whether or not with unalloyed regret, the world as it developed over the years since I first knew him.

But their significance for me will always be that when I had little hope of succeeding in the vocation I longed to pursue, they spoke to me of the quality of my ambitions, if not of their possibility. At a time between feminisms, in the dreariest decades for women of the twentieth century, Fadiman, Trilling, and Barzun invigorated and encouraged one woman who could never join their club, but who learned from them certain truths about the intellectual life, as well as the virtues of uneasy but honorable endeavors.

Bibliography

Anderson, Quentin, Stephen Donadio, and Steven Marcus, eds. *Art, Politics, and Will: Essays in Honor of Lionel Trilling.* New York: Basic Books, 1977.

Barzun, Jacques. *Berlioz and His Century: An Introduction to the Age of Romanticism.* New York: Meridian Books, 1956. Reprint with a new preface Chicago: University of Chicago Press, 1982.

———. *The Energies of Art: Studies of Authors Classic and Modern.* New York: Harper, 1956.

———. *From Dawn to Decadence: 500 Years of Cultural Life, 1500 to the Present.* New York: HarperCollins, 2000.

———. *The House of Intellect.* New York: Harper and Row, 1959.

———. *Race: A Study in Superstition.* New York: Harper and Row, 1965.

———. "Remembering Lionel Trilling." *Encounter* 47, 3 (September 1976): 82–88.

———. *A Stroll with William James.* New York: Harper and Row, 1983.

———. *Teacher in America.* Boston: Little, Brown, 1945. Reprint Indianapolis: Liberty Press 1981.

———. *The Use and Abuse of Art.* Bollingen Series 35; A. W. Mellon Lectures in the Fine Arts. Princeton, N.J.: Princeton University Press, 1974.

Barzun, Jacques and Henry F. Graff. *The Modern Researcher.* 5th ed. Boston: Houghton Mifflin, 1992.

Barzun, Jacques and Wendell Hertig Taylor. *A Catalogue of Crime.* New York: Harper and Row, 1971.

———, eds. *Classic Short Stories of Crime and Detection.* New York: Garland, 1983.

Brooks, David. *Bobos in Paradise: The New Upper Class and How They Got There.* New York: Simon and Schuster, 2000.

Dickstein, Morris. *Gates of Eden: American Culture in the Sixties.* New York: Basic Books, 1977.

Donadio, Stephen. Interview with Lionel Trilling. "Columbia: Seven Interviews." *Partisan Review* (Summer 1968): 386–92.

———. "Black Power at Columbia." *Commentary* 46, no. 3 (September 1968): 67–76.

Fadiman, Anne. *Ex Libris: Confessions of a Common Reader.* New York: Farrar Straus, 1998.

Fadiman, Clifton. *Any Number Can Play.* Cleveland: World, 1957.

———. *Enter Conversing.* Cleveland: World, 1962.

———. "Lionel Trilling and the Party of the Imagination." *New York,* April 22, 1950, 115–18.

———, ed. *Living Philosophies: The Reflections of Some Eminent Men and Women of Our Time.* New York: Doubleday, 1990.

———. *Party of One: The Selected Writings of Clifton Fadiman.* Cleveland: World, 1955.

———. *Reading I've Liked: A Personal Selection.* New York: Simon and Schuster, 1941.

Frank, Joseph. "Lionel Trilling and the Conservative Imagination." In Frank, *The Widening Gyre: Crisis and Mastery in Modern Literature.* New Brunswick, N.J.: Rutgers University Press, 1963. 253–72.

Greene, Gayle and Coppélia Kahn. *Changing Subjects: The Making of Feminist Literary Criticism.* New York: Routledge, 1993.

Grumet, Elinor. "The Apprenticeship of Lionel Trilling." *Prooftexts* 4 (1984): 153–73.

Howe, Irving. "On Lionel Trilling." *New Republic,* March 13, 1976, 29–31.

"An Interview with Clifton Fadiman." Oral History Research Office, Columbia University, 1955.

Jacobson, Dan. "Beyond Whose Culture?" *Commentary* (March 1966): 87–93.

James, Henry. *The Short Stories of Henry James.* Ed. and intro. Clifton Fadiman. New York: Random House, 1945.

Kazin, Alfred. *New York Jew.* New York: Knopf, 1978. Reprint Syracuse, N.Y.: Syracuse University Press, 1996.

Krupnick, Mark. *Lionel Trilling and the Fate of Cultural Criticism.* Evanston, Ill.: Northwestern University Press, 1986.

Krutch, Joseph Wood. *More Lives Than One*. New York: William Sloane, 1962.

Krystal, Arthur. "Five Centuries' Worth of Facts on the Best-Seller List." *New Yorker*, June 19, 2000, 74.

Kumin, Maxine. "October 4, 1995." In Kumin, *Always Beginning: Essays on a Life in Poetry*. Port Townsend, Wash.: Copper Canyon Press, 2000. 57–64.

Laskin, David. *Partisans: Marriage, Politics, and Betrayal Among New York Intellectuals*. New York: Simon and Schuster, 2000.

Lesser, Wendy. "Recollected in Tranquility." *American Scholar* (Winter 2000): 134–40.

Marcus, Steven. "Lionel Trilling, 1905–1975." *New York Times Book Review*, February 8, 1976, 1–3.

Marder, Herbert. *The Measure of Life: Virginia Woolf's Last Years*. Ithaca, N.Y.: Cornell University Press, 2000.

Moi, Toril. *What Is a Woman? and Other Essays*. New York: Oxford University Press, 1999.

Ozick, Cynthia. "The Buried Life." *New Yorker*, October 2, 2000, 116–26.

Radway, Janice A. *A Feeling for Books: The Book-of-the-Month Club, Literary Taste and Middle-Class Desire*. Chapel Hill: University of North Carolina Press, 1997.

Ravitch, Diane. *Left Back: A Century of Failed School Reforms*. New York: Simon and Schuster, 2000.

Rodden, John, ed. *Lionel Trilling and the Critics: Opposing Selves*. Lincoln: University of Nebraska Press, 1999.

Rothstein, Edward. "A Sojourner in the Past Retraces His Steps." *New York Times*, April 15, 2000, B7, B9.

Scott, A. O. "A Finished Woman." *New York Review of Books*, September 21, 2000.

Senett, Richard. "On Lionel Trilling." In *Lionel Trilling and the Critics: Opposing Selves*, ed. John Rodden. Lincoln: University of Nebraska Press, 1999. 359–66.

Slesinger, Tess. *The Unpossessed*. 1934. Reprinted as *The Unpossessed: A Novel of the Thirties*. Intro. Alice Kessler-Harris and Paul Lauter, Afterword Janet Sharistanian. Old Westbury, N.Y.: Feminist Press, 1984.

Tanenhaus, Sam. "When Left Turns Right, It Leaves the Middle Muddled." *New York Times*, September 16, 2000, B7–9.

Trilling, Diana. *The Beginning of the Journey: The Marriage of Diana and Lionel Trilling*. New York: Harcourt Brace, 1993.

———. *Claremont Essays*. New York: Harcourt, Brace and World, 1964.

———. "Lionel Trilling: A Jew at Columbia." *Commentary* (March 1979): 40–46.

———. *Mrs. Harris: The Death of the Scarsdale Diet Doctor.* New York: Harcourt Brace Jovanovich, 1981.

———. *We Must March My Darlings: A Critical Decade.* New York: Harcourt Brace Jovanovich, 1977.

Trilling, James. "My Father and the Weak-Eyed Devils." *American Scholar* (Spring 1999): 17–41.

Trilling, Lionel. *Beyond Culture: Essays on Literature and Learning.* New York: Viking, 1965.

———. *E. M. Forster.* Norfolk, Conn.: New Directions, 1943. Reprint New York: Harcourt Brace 1971.

———. *Freud and the Crisis of Our Culture.* Boston: Beacon Press, 1955.

———. "From the Notebooks of Lionel Trilling." *Partisan Review* 4 (1984): 496–515; Part II, 5 (1985): 7–17.

———. *A Gathering of Fugitives.* Boston: Beacon Press, 1956. Reprint New York: Harcourt Brace Jovanovich, 1978.

———. Introduction to Jane Austen, *Emma.* Riverside edition. Boston: Houghton Mifflin, 1957.

———. *The Last Decade: Essays and Reviews, 1965–75.* Ed. Diana Trilling. New York: Harcourt Brace Jovanovich, 1979.

———. *The Liberal Imagination: Essays on Literature and Society.* New York: Viking, 1951. Reprint New York: Harcourt Brace Jovanovich, 1979.

———. *The Middle of the Journey.* New York: Viking, 1947. Reprint with an introduction by the author New York: Harcourt Brace, 1975.

———. *Mind in the Modern World.* New York: Viking, 1972.

———. *The Opposing Self: Nine Essays in Criticism.* New York: Viking, 1955. Reprint New York: Harcourt Brace, 1978.

———. *Prefaces to The Experience of Literature.* New York: Harcourt Brace Jovanovich, 1967. Reprint 1979.

———. *Sincerity and Authenticity.* Cambridge, Mass.: Harvard University Press, 1972.

———. *Speaking of Literature and Society.* Ed. Diana Trilling. New York: Harcourt Brace Jovanovich, 1980.

———. "Young in the Thirties." *Commentary* (May 1966): 43–51.

Van Doren, Mark. *The Autobiography of Mark Van Doren.* New York: Greenwood Press, 1958.

Warshaw, Robert. "The Legacy of the Thirties." In *Lionel Trilling and the Critics: Opposing Selves*, ed. John Rodden. Lincoln: University of Nebraska Press, 1999.

———. Review of Lionel Trilling, *The Middle of the Journey*. *Commentary* (December 1947).

Weiner, Dora B. and William K. Keylor, eds. *From Parnassus: Essays in Honor of Jacques Barzun*. New York: Harper and Row, 1976.

Wharton, Edith. *Ethan Frome*. New York: Scribner's, 1911. Reprint with an Afterword by Alfred Kazin. New York: Simon and Schuster, 1997.

Wilkinson, Ellen. *The Division Bell Mystery*. 1932. Reprint New York: Garland, 1976.

Woolf, Virginia. *To the Lighthouse*. 1927. Reprint San Diego: Harcourt Brace Jovanovich, 1990.

INDEX